FISHING
for DREAMS

NOTES from the
WATER'S EDGE

D. C. Reid

TouchWood Editions
#108 – 17665 66A Avenue
Surrey, BC Canada V3S 2A7
www.touchwoodeditions.com

Library and Archives Canada Cataloguing in Publication
Reid, D. C. (Dennis C.), 1952-
          Fishing for dreams: notes from the water's edge / D.C. Reid.

ISBN 1-894898-28-1

          1. Fishing—British Columbia. 2. Fishing—Alberta. I. Title.

SH571.R44 2005   799.1'09711   C2005-901724-4

Edited by Marlyn Horsdal
Cover and book design by Erin Woodward
Front cover photo by Mark White

Printed in Canada

TouchWood Editions acknowledges the financial support for its publishing
program from the Government of Canada through the Book Publishing Industry
Development Program (BPIDP), Canada Council for the Arts, and the British
Columbia Arts Council.

*This book has been produced on 100% recycled paper, processed chlorine free and printed
with vegetable-based inks.*

Contents

"Angling is somewhat like poetry, men are to be born so."

–Izaak Walton

Acknowledgments

My thanks go to Elizabeth and John Johnston, owners of Tyee Lodge, Bamfield; Mark White, brilliant photographer; Peter Hovey, laconic guide to fishing among Swiftsure Bank mountains; Morgan McLean, who took me out on several occasions and demonstrated his fly finesse with the steelhead who swam through it; Doug Ferguson, Bamfield, who has the most bullet-shaped salted-herring rig in the world; Mike Coyne, manager of Tasu Lodge in the Queen Charlotte Islands; George Cuthbert, manager of Estevan Group Lodge and then Englefield Bay, Queen Charlotte Islands; Peter Bueschkens, storyteller and manager of Redfern River Lodge; Bill von Brendel, guide, who fishes with more intensity than anyone I know; Gerry Frederick, who took me to that gem of a river, the Wigwam in the East Kootenays; Gord Coutts, neighbour and competent captain of *Ocean Investor*, with whom I saw the day come twice; Kenneth Bejcar, manager of Wilp Syoon lodge; Dwayne D'Andrea, guide, who Huckleberry-Finned me down the Columbia River; Patrick Lane, poet and fisher dude; Terri Yamagishi, soft-spoken editor of the Japanese version of *Fly Fishing in Saltwaters;* Martin Paish, of Oak Bay Marine Group; Tracey Ellis, George Greuenefeld, Neil Cameron and Karl Bruhn (who gave me my start in the fishing magazine world), editors of *BC Outdoors;* Nick Amato, editor of *Salmon Trout Steelheader;* Chris Marshal, editor of *Canadian Fly Fisher;* Patrick Walsh, editor of *Outdoor Canada;* and Marlyn Horsdal, who edited this book.

Introduction

When I was three, I began to wander. Much to my parents' frustration, dismay and relief I was found one time, just before they were to embark on a vacation to Hawaii, propping up a wall next to the old White Rose gas pump with its calibrated glass container on top and bubbles rising. My precocious response was an irascible, "I know where I am."

Thus it began. By five, I had broken free. From the neighbourhood and from Calgary. Sixteenth Avenue was little more than a tarred trail past 19th Street where we lived and I emerged to look over endless yellow prairie and the most enduring blue sky. No 24th Street, no football stadium, no Foothills Hospital, just space for me to breathe in and pass into.

Before I began kindergarten, I was moving out into the land for miles, pillaging every small scrap of water of its frogs and bugs. And when I came to Bowness and the Bow River I could see what I wanted and knew I needed a rod and an old Johnson Century casting reel. My life since then has always been about water.

At 12, I, or rather we, moved to the cliff-top home above the first water I would call my own. And my territory doubled, fully 10 miles of wandering into my teenaged years in the sunburnt land of rolling Alberta hills. And then my first Volkswagen Beetle, of which you will hear more. And then my yellow canoe.

A friend and I foolishly began our tale of deliverance down the Bow River 50 miles in a blizzard. We dumped on the first corner and froze. The only smart thing we did was decide to go to the bar in Banff before shooting the falls. Serendipity had me come upon one of my previous girlfriends and she, lucky for us, saved our lives by letting us "crash," as all youth say, with her. The next morning, we surveyed the falls from above, and realized they were five times as long as they looked from up- or downriver.

From many scrapes I moved even farther away, west, to my present home of Victoria. I gave up the limitless prairie sky for pungent saltwater and the miracle of tide, coming in, going out. Thence began more than a score of years' introduction to salt water salmon fishing — I didn't have enough money for freshwater gear as well.

Frequently, over the years, when I told someone how to catch a salmon, he would say, "You should write about fishing." My response was, "Oh, sure," because what made me think I knew anything as much as Charlie White, Alec Merriman, Lee Straight and so on? But one day, I decided to write a story about using tiny freshwater Snelled hooks for coho in the dark, their splats in the water creating green phosphorescent craters by disturbing the light-releasing plankton in the sea. That first story, much to my surprise, was published by Karl Bruhn in *BC Outdoors,* and is included here.

Then the writing about fishing began. To backtrack for a second though, one other side of my life is as a writer of literature: stories; poetry; and novels. Now I have four books of poetry published (another on the way), one novel (and two more on the way) and another fishing book, *How To Catch Salmon* (and another on the way). To me, writing non-fiction — in this book's case, literary non-fiction — is like breathing. While it's necessary, one doesn't give breathing a second thought; it comes automatically and carries on, flooding your lungs and heart and brain all day every day into the years.

So, this book that you have comes from an artesian side of my nature and that is writing *true,* well somewhat true, *real* stories. A writer does two things: understands the high points of reality that set a story to its advantage, and extends the truth a little to make those high points interesting. A writer does not think too much about the writing; it comes, as I have said, like lungs welcoming the Earth's air.

I have kept my abiding interest in fishing, in wandering and in breathing. This book attends to some of the many places I have wandered in search of fish. It is universal experience, regardless of the province, state or even country, in which the fishing takes place. Our reasons for the pursuit of fish are our own, but we are united in an endless interest in the magic-making animals beneath our eyes in the secret water.

I have moved on to fish every which way, the six disciplines of gear, fly and Spey, in both salt- and freshwater. Please let this book of my wandering carry you along to spots in British Columbia and Alberta, from the east Kootenays and their cutthroat trout to the Queen Charlotte Islands for all species of salmon, and ling cod longer than a net; to the interior plateau rainbow country, and down the entire west coast — all fisheries that I have been fortunate, as a sport-fishing journalist, to be asked to attend. And I strove endlessly to catch them fishies. I get no sympathy for my efforts from others and my response is always the same: just because I enjoy it doesn't make it not work ... if you follow my drift. No? Well then, read on.

Thank you for entering my world of fishing; please feel free to make it your own.

Why I Fish and Do Not Hunt

Reaching into the invisible and pulling out the beautiful. This is fishing's greatest appeal. It is magic, an art form. At its most basic, this art is about killing another animal and the speeding of the heart that attends. And thus it is religion, for we must give thanks to the fish for surrendering its body for our tooth and mind to appreciate.

And when the last fish is killed, true appreciation begins; in my own life, the *Star Trek* Klingon stilled after 10,000 deaths. Now, I think this creature deserves its one life more than it deserves to have it removed. It deserves better than to have its body retained until freezer burn eliminates its taste and then thrown out without being consumed. It deserves life.

My view of life, how it works, comes from the most important things that I have learned. My first university degree is in zoology and biochemistry, a B.Sc. The great secret of these areas of human thought is a book of colour thrown open. From that open book is read the construction of life and the meaning of life. I was taught to understand life on a molecular level, and thus how the world of carbon and hydrogen and oxygen and nitrogen works to conjure life from elements that contain none.

Another great illumination is the evolution of species. Through the entire vertebrate world — fish, frogs, snakes, birds and mammals — with minor differences, the same, anti-diuretic hormone molecule regulates the removal of water from the blood in the kidneys. The retention of one chemical is repeated in thousands of chemicals across the entire world of animals with backbones. This was a major revelation for me and helped prove to me that evolution of species is simply a fact; those who argue for divine intervention — not necessarily a Christian God — are simply incorrect. Every living thing can be explained in terms of its material of reproduction: DNA, deoxyribonucleic acid, from viruses (with the exception of a few that have RNA) up to man. A mouse and a man have more than 90 percent of the same genetic material.

I do not quarrel with those who are religious. It is clear to me that religion, along with self-awareness, language and economy, is one of the most important aspects of our sentience. Religion is important as all humans seek some way to explain the origins of life, our nature in life, a sense of law and morality and the nature of objects around us as well as what happens to living things when the form they are in dies and is degraded.

I am thus, as philosophers may wish to phrase my views, a soft biological determinist. As I see it, there is nothing beyond the physical. Thought is the function of the organ called the brain. I do not think my view is difficult to understand and it is not disagreeable to many people. It includes the knowledge that sentience is the result of a physical organ. Without the organ there is no self-awareness. A rock, then, is not aware of itself.

Now that my view and its underpinnings have been sketched, it is time to move to the first time I remember catching a fish. I was five and my family was out at an office party along a stream. Two men came up and said that there was a trout under a rock they would like to catch. They asked me to help. When they lifted the rock and the trout had to slither away in half an inch of water, I was supposed to grab it and they would take it. They had a large outdoor pool and other fish assembled there over the years. I would be allowed to come along and see it.

So, the two of them hunkered down, hands upon a rock the size of a small ottoman. I squatted across the trickle of water flowing from under the rock. When they lifted, the trout squirted out and when it went past me, I reached into the stream and pulled it out. Just like that: no emotion, no prescience of what fish would come to mean to me later in life. It is no great hyperbole to say that fish now rule my life.

But though I felt no emotion about the fish other than possessiveness, I would not give it up to the men for their keeping in a large tank in their car. I would not honour the bargain that I had struck. No. Instead, I would take it home and keep it myself. Reluctantly, they put it in the squat relish bottle I presented. The fish was far too large for the small bottle and simply bent around the inside, unable to move. I can still see the image of the fish stuck in the bottle. Nevertheless, I was resolute in standing against the men and my parents.

Crying, unwilling to give up the fish, I had it transferred to the roaster in which we cooked the Sunday beef. By the time we got home the fish was leaning off centre. As I have come to know, the effort to stay upright is a deep instinct for a fish. One that cannot maintain its balance is going to die. I recall being in tears watching the fish for the rest of the afternoon, watching it lose ground and lose ground until it was upside down, belly-up in the roaster.

I knew that I had done something truly shameful. And that I had been wrong. Had I given the fish to the men it would have happily survived and I could have visited if I wished. Instead, my intransigence had resulted in death. Fish are not puppets suspended on silky strings. They are magic, in their dance within the liquid air, the red of their fan-shaped gills opening to take in life. This magic I had destroyed.

To the present day, I recall this incident and will always do so. I do not feel ashamed anymore, but I remember. I did the wrong thing. I killed another living being at five years of age. It was a bad surprise; I had not realized it would happen. And yet it did.

Also in the early days, I remember going with my father and some other men in a large, dark, 1950s-era car. I rode in silence deep in the back seat and later the men talked among themselves as we moved out along a brown trail. We walked into a forest where a stream flowed among the roots. Memory does not give me anyone with fishing gear, though a small trout was angled. It was put into my hand and I remember being hooked from that moment and in every moment that has followed. That a fish was invisible in knee-deep water was wondrous and I had to have them myself.

Sweat dripping down my chin and itching up my shirt, I watched the rainbow colours disappear as home we drove on the hot summer day. The fish was a hard glass corpse by the time we arrived and when cooked, its flesh I refused to eat. Since that day I have fished with greater and greater intensity. And it is the intensity of expectation, even when one is thrashed and truly beaten, that is the lure of fishing. There is no enjoyment of the summer day for me. For more than a couple score years it was the gambler's sweat of possibility, the connection to the pleasure centre of the brain, that explained my attachment to fishing.

I have read what the great writers have written and find their reasons not among my own. I have read and read the long, the involved, the high, the moral, the lofty, the etc. Read Dame Berners and Izaak Walton for the reasons of fishing's allure. In her *The Treatyse on Fysshynge with an Angle,* 1496, the Dame recommends fishing "pryncypally for your solace and to cause the helthe of your body and specially of your soule." Walton, in his happy little volume *The Compleat Angler,* further observed, in 1653, "Its solitary recreation banishes idleness and allows time for serious and holy contemplation."

I find none of that. I make the argument that fishing is the finest form of battle. And the moment of fish in the sky under tension to the tip is battle of greatest purity. But to call it purity is to overlook the biological facts. My understanding of the world is of its molecules, its serotonin, amygdala, cell membrane potentials and nerves that work by the sodium and potassium ion pumps. Unless all those work, there is no pleasure in the centre of the brain. I am one whose wiring receives so much nervous anticipation that I cannot sleep before going fishing, that in my 50s I still wake before the alarm clock rings (and cannot leave the alarm clock off because I cannot sleep, worrying all night that I'll be asleep when it is time to go).

And, of course, fishing is reckless gambling. You place your money, the ball totters among the catching cups and then it lands. If you are right, it pays 35 to 1. But as we all know, the odds are stacked against you. Slowly you lose and keep on losing, all the while keeping hope that you will win. Such is the mind set of the addicted gambler and so it is of the angler. And that is what fishing is to me: it is an addiction, one of great pleasure. And it is more: it is part of my identity. Part of who I am. Beyond the biological purpose of reproducing one of one's kind, which is life's only purpose (consider that if there were no need for reproduction, we would never be born, and life could never have evolved), I was put here to catch fish, and I do that. And that truly is something large and important. For the hardwiring of personality presents the opportunity to find out who you are and to do what your mind tells you to do in this one finite chance at life. In current psychology-speak, if you know what your feelings are and you know why you have those feelings then you must act in accord with them to be fulfilled.

Fishing is fulfilment of who I am. Examination of the motives that move me to fish leads on to examining why I make it the focus of my life; that is, the rest of my life is organized around fishing. Each year I catch and release more than 500 salmon. I do this because doing fishing is doing me. Doing Dennis — the best thing that I can do. I do not think about fishing, per se, I do not think about the river or the ocean because my focus is on catching the fish before me. If one does what one is set on this Earth to do, then one has happily achieved something far too few people manage in this short, one-time entry into the existent. I am completely absorbed in the environment and the techniques of fly and gear in an effort to understand and reap the rewards of a beautiful wild creature that I appreciate and then send along its way unharmed.

When I fish, the boundary between nature and me disappears. I am simply another part of it, not a man isolated from his source. I have never felt outside of or distinct from nature. The view that the world of man is separate from the world of nature is not my view. What I do feel, instead, is that the world of humans has lost its way if it cannot be a part of the world that engenders and surrounds it. It is an existence that is unhappy. Consider the question: is it better to die or never have existed at all, that union of sperm and egg finagled by your mother and father? Let me answer that it is better to exist and die, though death is an unhappy eventuality for those who live and for all those who know them.

I am often asked whether I hunt. And I suppose, when you fish as I do, it is a form of hunting. Knowledge built up over decades makes one far more capable of drawing a bead on a fish. This fine knowledge includes fish behaviour and water, with its hydraulic considerations. It grants me the chance to fool the predatory instinct of fish, who are carnivores by and large and seek out and eat what they want. Strangely, a spinner, a Vibrax Blue Fox, Bolo or whatever, does not even resemble a kind of food and yet a fish will follow, be stimulated by and glom the lure. I have had unhooked fish refuse to give up a spinner blade until they were in the net, even though it didn't look, taste or feel like real food.

I am a hunter of fish. When I was a boy in Calgary, every boy in the country, and most in the city, had a gun. It was common for kids to be seen on the wastelands with a BB gun, a small air-compression weapon, often shaped like a Winchester. Loading the barrel, as in a shotgun, you pumped the barrel and compressed the air so when the trigger was pulled a round copper pellet fired.

I had a pellet gun, a rifle much more powerful than a BB gun. I also had a 22, which fired a single, gunpowder-propelled lead bullet. Open the breach, insert the bullet, slide in the bolt, put the gun on safety and pull back fully, then crack, the gun reported across the 1950s and early '60s prairie, its grey and yellow, its snow in the lee of the wolf willow, crocus gaping before the last snow left the land.

At that time, gophers (a small, social ground squirrel) were considered vermin and a bounty of five cents was paid for each tail. Taking the life of an animal was worth only a nickel and I was a very good shot. Gophers were considered bad because their holes, sometimes a foot or two across, and tailings, stretching in a six- to eight-foot circle, were said to result in broken legs for horses. So they said. I paid for my bullets easily by killing gophers and then had money for other things. A diminutive bounty hunter, you could say.

One day, I looked down the unused well behind our house that filled almost to the surface every spring. I discovered a wet gopher, scrabbling at the inside walls of the foot-wide pipe. It would swim until it drowned. That was the only outcome. Or I could shoot it. But I didn't think of the option of putting it out of its misery. I just went into the house and in the night, when I was wakeful, knew that while I was safe and warm that animal was dying. I have no memory of going back to check on it. It was an irrelevant death and a small tragedy.

In a boy's careless brutality, I learned to hunt efficiently. I learned to aim low so the malleable bullet would bounce from the ground distorted and thus on entry mushroom up into the animal in a broader shape that would be more effective in killing. When I was about 13, I had pretty much stopped shooting gophers. Without moral qualms about what I had done, I moved on to a different use for my guns, but the last death crystallized my mind; never again could I kill with a gun.

Walking east in grasses that swished my knees to the ravine leading down to Fish Creek where the cliffs had worn away and were just a hill, I was attracted by the song of a sparrow, its black feet wrapping the wire of the barbed-wire fence. I took aim at that sparrow and when the shot rang out it fell from the wire and plopped within the swaying timothy and brome. I had shot off the roof of its skull and it lay in the grasses far away from itself, small convoluted brain beating in a light pink fluid. I knew immediately, and deeply, that I had done a great wrong that could not be righted. That was the last animal I shot, and though the purpose of hunting is to procure meat, I found I could never again take aim at a warm animal. My shooting was restricted to popping screws out of fence posts over the cliffs and shooting the stalks of Queen Anne's Lace so they would fall over. One day, I put the barrel of the gun in a vice and hit it with a hammer so that it would never again kill anything. The bolt I threw from the cliff into what was left of my childhood.

These decades later, I have no issue with others who want to bring a moose or bear or elk or goose home to the kitchen table. That is their right. Hunting for food is legitimate and lawful. So while I cannot hunt, I have no dispute with those who want to.

My dispute, my quiet resistance, is with those who tell us we ought not hunt or fish. People who don't like a certain activity or outcome are allowed to have their view. But political correctness is all about crossing a fundamental boundary. That is the boundary between what I like or do not like and telling the rest of society they must feel and act the same way. Animal-rights activists extend their argument from themselves to society when they suggest that hunting and fishing are immoral and abusive to animals, particularly if the fisherman (the more enlightened and ethical of us) releases his catch.

It is suggested that killing an animal, a grizzly bear for instance, is morally repugnant and should be stopped. My answer to this line of reasoning is that it is manipulative. The way to deal with the actions of others is to accept and respect their right to do as they lawfully wish. It is of interest to me that this method of dealing with one's feelings is in essence existential. Psychoanalysis has much to thank Jean-Paul Sartre for and his concepts of "Good Faith" and "Bad Faith." If someone has an opposing view, I am not angered, I do not want them to change.

We live in a world, now, where most of us never have the life of another creature in our hands. We do not regularly kill. Remember, though, that before the 1950s most people had their own cows and chickens and when they wanted a dinner, they butchered an animal. Every person knew that today's roast came from a stunned cow strung up by the sinews of its hind leg, its throat slashed so the blood could seep out in its copiousness. That is the way of the world. For many things to live, they must kill other animals or plants. But over the decades, the activity of butchering has more and more become the basis of business rather than a killing each of us must do. And today more than 2.5 million cattle are slaughtered each year in Canada alone. This does not include chickens, hogs, sheep and other animals.

And we avoid the killing. I could not stand being in an abbatoir even for an hour. Our meat comes to us sanitized, in clinical foam trays, with bright labels for payment. The meat is clean, neat, attractive. No guts. No hair disfiguring the cut. No sawdust. No shit. We have become separated from ourselves, separated from the reality that living necessitates killing. Thus today, those who wish others to stop killing fish or other animals can sway opinion because all of us have become distanced from the killing our lives necessarily involve.

For me, there is an irony. While I say if you don't wish to eat meat, don't, I also don't eat meat, but not for any moral reason. I am allergic to meat and cannot eat it. I say, accept what others do and accept what you do. I will continue fishing. I will continue letting 98 percent of the fish I catch go and feeling guilt for killing the ones I retain. I have never met a fish that wanted me to kill it. How many do you think want to be let go?

Join me at the riverbank. Join me with your fly and your eyes searching the braiding elements. We will go back to being kids, when summer days lasted forever and every fish was a mystery and a sudden beating of the heart. Let us enjoy the odd truth that of what we remember, none comes from the past. Each time we think of the fish that tried us, we are, so the scientists now tell us, conjuring an image from one part of the brain with sensations from another, and the effect on our emotions is brought to a peak the moment we think it by the small almond of the brain, the amygdala, that assembles our memories in the present though we think of them as from the past. We still think of our complete thoughts as engrams, as was thought in the times of Orwell or Huxley, in their totalitarian literature. Some things are not as we think, and that is not a bad thing.

Back to Being a Kid in the Good Ol' Summertime

Sometimes, in the dog days of summer, when sun is a membrane on heads and hands and draws from bodies a slim layer of sweat, I abandon all pretense of being adult. I go back to being a kid. I resurrect the tried and true, the simple methods of catching fish, the strategies devised when summer was a sun-burned neck and day was dawn until dusk on Fish Creek or anywhere my casting reel and taped-up rod would slip its thread to the world beneath my eyes.

That siren of the past: memory. And a past remembered by an adult who knows that there is nothing intrinsically true and real in this world because his/my childhood has disappeared. That is how we grow. We understand that we are not real, that as the years pass only a few others remember our childhood. Now, some of us are gone and in short days all will be gone. Such an odd perspective, to be middle-aged and understand I am not completely real. And my memory fails, and my lenses become *progressive* — 50-year-old eyes no longer focus close and far away.

My gear leans against my parents' garage, the rods that spiders make chandeliers in the slanting evening light. The dinghy is pulled down the beach. On the southernmost tip of Vancouver Island, Saanich Inlet is home to the calmest waters in British Columbia. At 18 miles long and 750 feet deep, it ranks right up there with the longest and the deepest. Protected by the Malahat ridge on the west, Saanich Peninsula on the east and Salt Spring Island at its mouth, it presents a huge natural fish trap. Fish, meaning the relentlessly structure-related chinook, on their homeward migration south, swim down one shore, then turn at Goldstream River and come up the other side. Heading north for so many miles confuses these creatures of casual beauty, brains the size of fingernails; they turn back south, and thus become trapped in a net as open as a catcher's mitt.

So many times an amber remembrance: a trout under the cottonwood trees below the water intake for the Canyon Meadows golf course in Calgary. Seed sifted through the sun, filling the lee of bushes and the snake-hot rocks of the cliffs below our house where prairie falcons kri-kried their disapproval of my trying to put a blob of worm past the nose of the trout. Just opening triangular gills, calling all life into its body, it mesmerized me. Fish are enchantment and I was a fisherman, doing what all fishermen have always done: succumb to what they wish to understand.

And with the same odd feeling of déjà vu, as an adult, I watch schools of coho pass under my boat. These fish swim in an absolutely horizontal plane, almost touching, in schools of a score or more, unlike chinook; those more solitary individuals are driven by instinct to be in the same place at the same time and thus appear to be a school. Amazing the behaviour of animals, and what we can know. For instance, what does it mean, *what is its purpose,* that evolution has given us intelligence and the apparent freedom to choose our paths, unlike the coho below, oblivious to my Stingsilda.

Later, heat mist oozes from the land and rises on the water like an invisible hand signalling the moist dark mouth of night. The sun retrieves its tentacles over the Malahat ridge. Now is the time for the best, most true to the endless-summer promise, Huckleberry Finn, toe-dangling fish'n' that is mooching with just-raked, 2 ½-inch herring.

At other times of the day, chinook descend from a moochable 25 feet deep at the crack of dawn to as deep as 250 feet along the 50-fathom contour. And the traditional gear is fished, the wire line and roller-guided Peetz rods and their matching, from-another-era, six-inch wooden recorder reels that leave a burn from fingertip to heel of palm when a big fish goes.

But in the evening, in a few spots, fish nose the surface: Wain Rock, the spar buoy off Coles Bay and, on the Mill Bay side, Tanner and Tozier rocks. Some spots fish well in the middle of the night. The Bamberton shore in front of the old cement factory is lit like Cape Kennedy and the herring gather in galaxies, dimpling the water. At three in the morning it is an experience of another kind to watch the surface ripple into growing skin. On one side, herring flip as though tossed from the water and on the other, as confetti, shot from a canon. There is no sound except for the raindrop of their tiny bodies hitting the black. Lines astern, other boats rise from the dark and just as quickly fall back into it.

For the not-so-dogged fisher, for the soft fisher, for the Hamlet, in-terior-looking fisher, shallow-line mooching is food for thinking. The shallow-line spots attract clouds of newly hatched herring that pulse in their own twist where one and now another jags in a spiral, producing points of starlight.

On any evening you may find me crunching my dinghy across the gravel, crossing starfish and barnacles snatching at life. On the next dock stands the neighbour's kid, baseball cap turned back on his head, wiping fish blood on his jeans. He stuffs a baseball bat into a bucket of water. The bucket holds sole he's caught and chopped to pieces. He chums the water to lure 30-pound sharks that come curving, green eyed and prehistoric. He waves and baits his hook with half a sole. "They'll be here in 15 minutes," he says and points a finger below the float. Then he stoops over, eyes intent on the water: *The Fisherman*, the statue Rodin forgot to sculpt.

In my little boat, I bend and draw, bend and draw, stitching across the mirror of Coles Bay. The opposite shore and its reflection are a ballerina on toe. I pass the mansion of Myfanwy Pavelic, the famous artist who painted a devilish Trudeau with his rose and turned-up collar. Then I pass Dyer Rock where I once caught a 25-pound salmon and didn't have a net. I row and row. Land and its concept of restraint drop behind me: the office, the kids, the wife, the fax machine, the email.

I'm the same 12-year-old kid on the edge of his understanding, with the same gambler's optimism, en route to the simplest fishing I'll do this year. One 6-foot trout rod, 18-pound test, a couple of 1-ounce rubbercore weights and — brace yourself — some size 10 Snelled freshwater trout hooks. All around, Bonaparte gulls arc and turn, giving substance to the air. They touch the water, and rise, mouths whiskered with herring.

I take out my rake, made years ago by slicing a paddle blade and scarfing on a 10-foot extension. On its leading edge I mounted piano-wire pins. Each year I retrieve it from the rafters where it waits for August purpose. I raise it over my head and slice the water. Herring drop wriggling into the boat.

A Palomar knot secures the tiny hook to the Chameleon, fish-can't-see-the-stuff monofilament necessary for this I-can-inspect-this-gear-all-night-before-I-bite fishery. A rubbercore weight twists on 6 feet from the hook. A 10-pound chinook splats down, and I think, "You're mine." I insert the barb through a herring's lower and upper jaw. The only thing holding it is the tip of its lips.

Shallow mooching is as easy as it sounds: let out 25 2-foot pulls and row, then stop. Row, then stop. The bait moves through the water in a slow crest and trough, rising on the row and twinkling and sinking on the stop. The line moves to the side followed by the rod tip and the reel. My fingers crunch in the handles. Then it's over. The fish is gone. This is the downside to light-line mooching.

The Bonapartes are visible air, white as linen on a summer wind. I follow them because they mark the location of the herring school that shimmers beneath the sea. They hover close to the green spar buoy that marks a reef rising from 650-foot depths to a spire two fathoms below the surface. Between here and the shore half a mile away, the bottom is flattish, 40 feet deep and covered cheek-by-jowl with sea cucumbers.

The sea is a tabletop. Walking on it seems no difficult feat. The concept of wind is impossible. It is an evening when extreme mooching is at its best, i.e., fishing invented by a kid. This is the time when I look up and say, yes, the light is fading. A few touch-and-run salmon have taken my offering. A good thing, I think; a salmon just touched is a salmon that keeps looking. I row and stop, row and stop. I am watching my rod when its tip rises from the weight being lifted. This is nirvana. The moocher's grail: a few seconds you savour, fish on the end of the line and it doesn't yet know.

I lower my tip and reel into resistance. I yank to set the tiny hook in the bony jaw. This is followed by a fish, the wave of it across the surface, and my line trying to keep up. One hundred yards before I can stuff the rod between my legs and row in pursuit, the line passing above my head over the bow and the rod on the run hitting me in the face and shoulders. Then it's gone, a large northern coho. There are things we can learn by looking into them. And then we can forget that we know them. For me, in this, I forget my learning that a fish that moves so fast the reel can hardly contain its spin, a fish that runs right under the surface, is a coho far more often than a chinook. The latter more frequently take the lure down to the dim green depths.

The sun takes itself over the Malahat and evening slips in behind. Perhaps the only things we can depend on: the Earth, the sun, the moon and how they circle and draw each other. I row and pause, following the herring through the dusk. I pick up a chinook about six pounds. Then the dusk grows thick and, still in shirt sleeves, I turn for shore. The evening bite starts a couple of hours before dark in Saanich Inlet and usually ends before the black part of night, a pattern I have come to recognize as a year-round phenomenon. Still, I trail my line over the tiny transom. Shore lights prick the dark.

Behind me, pan-sized splots of green trail into the dark. I always marvel at this quiet light-show of nature, the bioluminescent plankton glowing when disturbed. My wake stretches into a graceful green tail; I could be traversing the Phantom of the Opera's grotto.

In almost complete, swallowing dark, my reel screeches and a green line zings beside the boat, followed by more silence, then a burst of green. The green line cracks open in front of the dinghy, then arrows to the other side; in the dark, my rod yanks over, following it to my right. This is followed by another burst of green, then slack line, then a green burst behind me and taut line again. After 20 minutes of green-cratered darkness, a 13-pound northern coho gasps in the net in the bottom of the boat.

Astonished, panting, I row in silence, pass the long house on Yarrow Point, lighted like a ship in the dark. Then the artist's estate, with its narrow beach, its concrete pier and studio large as an indoor tennis court. It slides by in the drip of oars.

"It's real eerie when those big green eyes come out from under the dock," a voice says, and I almost startle out the other side of my boat. It's the kid next door. I hear the reel grind, see his hands lift into moonlight. He's caught five so far, releases them after he catches them, and then he does it again, a kind of game. He's been catching the same sharks for years. Throws in his sole to keep them coming back. I jump into the future and see him as a man, standing on the dock in the dark, compromised, adult, doing the same thing 20 years from now.

I pull to my own shore and green explodes under the dinghy, yanking me into right now: a shark in the shallows. When my heart returns, I'm still a kid again, amazed as always by nature, its simplicity and endlessness, the fish in my boat, threadbare dungarees, knowing that summer and the dream never end. It's still and always magic: a fish.

How Pat Quinn Lost
The Great One

Thinking back, it is easy to face the moment of truth. For if we are no longer threatened, we no longer fear. And if we do not fear, perhaps we can swagger just a little. There is no bravado at the time, no flinty-eyed Clint Eastwood, make my day, chewed-in-half cigar of a day. Instead, in real time, admitting my sins and looking for mercy, I swill back a glass or two of Scotch at 7:30 AM and settle into my usual routine in an airplane: keeping it in the air by sheer force of will. The blue summer day it rises into could be a passage to heaven for all I know. Into lovely deception the plane rises and turns to the Queen Charlotte Islands as I, revealing no terror, pick up the morning paper.

At least eight pages are devoted to under-the-microscope reportage of luring, playing, then losing the best player in the National Hockey League. All the drama of the morning tab: the offers; the agents; the lawyers; Gretzky, in his Seattle hotel, refusing the millions and eluding Pat Quinn. Apparently, the blame for depriving the fans of the westernmost franchise rests in Pat's large, insensitive hands.

Leaving the paper and the rest of the world behind, I board an even smaller plane for the trip to Langara Island at the tippy-top end of the Charlottes. It throttles up into Haida Gwaii, its mist-shrouded skies mystical in CBC documentaries. Today, mizzle hides mountains and muskeg as we scrape through air so thick we might as well be flying with eyes closed. And across a flattened sea, 10 feet above the water, head in fog, the Twin Otter obeys the commands of a man who doesn't know how close we come to the cliffs in my mind. When both pontoons settle into a skid, we are on target for the northern oasis: the M.V. *Charlotte Princess,* a 136-foot vessel that will be my home for the duration of this catch-and-release episode. It is 1996 and chinook retention has been eliminated — after clients have paid their money, and are justifiably angry.

I drop my bags on the deck and strain on a hot-yellow floater suit. Like a cross between Apollo 13 and Andy-Wharholian Rupert Bear, I waddle to my Fat Cat, a specially designed, beamy craft with a 60-hp Johnson. Immediately I am a kid and roar off at full blast, the boat blamming from crest to crest. The only part of me touching the boat is my hand on the throttle.

Soon, cutplugging at 15 pulls, a set-up delightfully simple compared with the downriggers and planers I employ on the south coast, I snag the first fish. Above me, in the wind-ravaged Sitka spruce, perch more eagles than Hitchcock could imagine. The green-speckled chinook weighs in at 15 pounds and is released without being brought from the water. Before the sun is extinguished, I have also released a 14-pounder, a 13-pounder and 3 coho between 8 and 10 pounds — fishing of a kind of which I have only dreamed.

Sifting like Scotch through ice, 11:00 PM sun ambers from the sky, and I turn back to home base. Almost before my head hits the pillow it is 4:30 AM and I am rolled from bed by the photographer sent along to catch a release. On the deck in the NASA gleam of floodlights, frozen herring crash into buckets, handfuls of salt splatter in. The sea wrinkles and slides.

As I round the first corner, a path through the kelp falls open and I cut to the fishing grounds. Bait and fingertips are sliced in the pre-dawn light. White-headed eagles are brooding aboriginal gods in invisible perches. Three rods are dispatched to the water as I steer — wired on adrenaline, the only way I know how to fish — past a glum, grey-haired guy in a red sou'wester, red bib and red boat. I read salmon after salmon on the fish-finding sounder. The sea soon gives up its first: coho. As they usually do, the coho swim in a tight formation. I turn and re-cross the school, receiving my first double header, then my second. With only a four-ounce banana weight to slow them down, the fish leap and leap from the water. And so do I. The ultimate moment is fish in the air, the greatest chance of failure and so the greatest thrill: under control and touching the untouchable creatures with whom we share an unheld heart.

From the distance comes a whitening. I slice bait, test it beside the boat. Then the whitening is growing. Up out of the dawn, directly at me, 30 miles an hour, like the galloping worms of *Dune*. I stand in the boat and fight the first pink salmon, slice the line at the hooks. I am standing in the very far beyond of the far beyond, yanking Palomars with my teeth as hundreds of dolphins clear the water, huge and clean, passing through me as though I'm not here. How fortunate to feel the indifferent rumblings of nature. A thrill of fear shivers through.

By the time I recover from this waking dream, the tide has begun pushing the fish past the point into a back eddy filled with bass. The bass blot the scope, porpoise the surface like black rain. To fish through them is to receive a fish on every line. Underneath are chinook and I persist; cutting bait, rigging, testing roll and letting out line.

The rod tip stabs the water and pulls me into the first big fish of my trek north. I brace my feet against the transom. This is why I have come, in a DFO season of catch and release. My job, my serious job is to be in photos releasing big ones. In his boat, the photographer yells for me to put on the glove. Left hand around the wrist of the fish's tail, right hand under its belly, I lean over the gunwale. One second I'm up to my armpits, next the sea pitches me and the 25-pounder clear of the water. After the photograph, the fish disappears in a tailsnap. Leaves me with my hands on my hips, thankful to have let such a large and vibrant creature free.

A Zodiac appears, its orange-toqued inhabitant snapping across the waves. Tea is offered, and biscuits, but no date with the queen; civilized fishing 500 miles from nowhere. A day of fish-till-you-drop excitement. At dinner, I am told I caught more fish than anyone else.

Over his glass of Chilean chardonnay, the captain says, "Here you are fishing three rods on your own. Slicing bait, rigging lines. Without looking up from the cutting board, you're steering in an absolutely straight line with your knee. You have a pair of pliers in your mouth and I watched you land a triple header, reaching down the line with one hand, pulling the pliers out with the other and snipping off the fish before it can twist up at the side of the boat."

Embarrassed, I realize that 40 years of fishing have given me the experience to do such things. And it's true, I seldom look where I am going, preferring to steer by the angle of the prop wash. And I look down at my plate. At the various poisons it contains. Over the years, I have grown allergies that flare like leprosy along my legs and underarms. Nuts, ice cream, beer, even the innocuous carrot. I do not mention that I have brought a bag of raison scones and dozens of apples. And then it's blue pills and yellow pills, the oblivion of sleep.

Then it's 4:30 AM and I drag my carcass into my hot-yellow suit, present my sleeping brain on the misty deck. This day we head to the halibut grounds. Full throttle through four-foot rollers, rear end six inches from my seat, kidneys hitting every trough. Four miles into the open Pacific. Four yellow Fat Cats in 250 feet of water, next stop Japan. Much to my surprise, I hook a 100-pound halibut on the first drop. The photographer hooks one so large his boat moves resolutely away, towing him like some astonished Spencer Tracy. The beast proves so large it can't be slowed. A quarter mile away, the 60-pound leader finally breaks. Around us grey whales breach like temporary islands, huge and barnacled, alien and intelligent.

Then I'm reclining in a hot tub, sipping Peruvian white. Above me the Sitka spruce bend like pushed-over minds. Eagles eye me hungrily, my warm pink flesh and the blotches on my arms and legs. Through the night the mist is in the hallways and the generator thrums against the dark. I am reminded of *Heart of Darkness,* Kurtz's thoughts festooned and capitulating in relentless jungle.

Then it's 4:30 AM and I'm yawning on the deck. Trays of herring are flung down, fists of salt thrown in. Zagging through the kelp, wake snapping 20 feet into the grey, I head once more to Cohoe Point. This proves a day of pinks, the erratic craziness of bite periods unrelated to tide. My hands are nicked and aching. I look up from cutting bait to the baleful stare of the grey-haired guy in his red sou'wester and bib. Whatever the reason, he is as lugubrious as a catfish. I position my boat to pass behind him and angle into the school. Pinks are bleeders and soft mouthed. Releasing them unnetted and in the sea is necessary. Every time I look up, the big man goes by, hands on his knees, watching me catch another one. Twelve feet across and nimble, an eagle reaches down a Godlike talon, plucking a grilse from the waters between us.

Then it's 4:30 AM. The last day. I'm so tired I can hardly put in the time until the plane. But we still need that trophy on film and I have to carry on. (Do I hear sympathy? No?) The fish have moved overnight to Gunia Point. In the early chop, I find a reef on the screen at 50 feet. It's covered with huge, black, simulated Pac-Man fish on the screen but not yet on the bite. The fleet motors down a mile, turns and putts its way back. Then the boats yaw out again. I stay over the reef, going in circles among the boats. And I am rewarded. I get a coho double header and am playing one while loosening the drag on the other when 20 feet away a minke whale breaches, smooth and dark. And then it is gone — like a memory.

Then the fish I've come for: a 35-pounder. I wave my Day-Glo blue hat and the photographer turns from the distance, readying his camera. This time my gloved hand can barely clear the wrist and I push it against the boat. The fish gasps in my arms, girth lying from my hand to my elbow. The boat drops and my head disappears in the sea. The flash lights the fishing ground like benign lightning. Baleful as ever, the red sou'wester glides by our impromptu movie set. As long as my leg, the fish hangs from my hand in the water. Then it drifts to another world, a reluctant warrior I have been allowed to touch.

It is now that I quit. I have caught 12 fish this morning. My next would be the 13th and I am catching a plane, so an extra is not to be risked. Thirty-five salmon have been caught and released. Eight halibut.

I stare down at my simple hands on the plane from Sandspit. There are dozens of nicks from the needle teeth of salmon. I can't form fists. Then a hand lands on the seat in front of me, fingers twice the size of mine. The hand is connected to an arm of equal heft and bone. A broad back, thick hips. A man who dwarfs me. A man with grey hair. I realize it is the man from the sea, not so old, in his 50s, but a huge man, intimidating. Then I realize it's Pat Quinn, and don't know what to say. So I don't say anything, to grant him anonymity. To save him from the question about Gretzky. But I think to myself: he would've landed The Great One if he'd brought him to this wilderness that is Canada. Perhaps he would've been happier in his quaint red hat.

Leaving My Life Behind

*During the day I laugh and during the night
I sleep
My favourite cooks prepare my meals,
my body cleans and repairs itself,
and all my work goes well.*
—Leonard Cohen, "I Have Not Lingered in
European Monasteries"

Leaving my life behind. What does this mean?
Something sinister? Something apocalyptic? And
what is left? My brown tabby cat for sure: Ted,
known also as Ted the Tuna Monster, having, in my
various absences, been fed so much tuna by my
good friend and cat keeper that he expects it out
of me all the time. So there is Ted. And there is
my constant companion: my computer. My line
to the world. I sit in my office on any old day,
staring at blue sky and palm trees, scanner, CD
abuzz with itself, two programs for receiving the
world on a 17-inch screen. Is it 40 gigs of hard drive?
Yes. So large it contains the hard drives of my four

previous computers and still has room for everything I will ever write, in this and any other universe, as they say in writing contracts.

One point eight gigahertz of speed, already obsolete by the time this story rests on paper in this book. We live our lives in an information river. A river we notice only when we are startled in the morning, in the window that gives back ourselves and we look in and say, that old person can't be me, I'm at the height of my life, 19, and able to pick up mooring rings that weigh more than I do.

But in that river we turn and roll through riffles, plumb waters so deep they're frightening. White water is the big issues: can we give birth; do we have enough money; is the bottle of wine too freely down a throat; do we one day look across the bed and say, I do not know this person in my life; and, do we ever get to know the person we are closest to — ourselves?

In my case, my younger years were spent on water, along the tunnel of green cottonwoods prodigious with their seeding of summer, and always taking chances, and never drowning for being too daring. "Yes, I can cross this river," then finding it too deep and too strong and being carried away, keeping my head above water, that is, living the issues of life. And I in head-on collision because I think it can never get the better of me.

That has humour, these scores of years later. I am risking death once more, in the summer British Columbia is on fire. What the pinewood beetles first destroy, the great mouth of fire consumes. Flying into Anahim, into a military operation on the strip. Eighteen stiff-winged, helicopter insects coming and going, tents for hundreds of men, trucks for hundreds more, the temporary fuel dump and the sound and smell of Vietnam. Choppers and smoke and rubber and aviation fuel.

And so the Beaver hacks its smoker's cough of diesel until it runs true. Coming in low to the blue lake of Eutsuk, pontoons 10 feet from the water, lines trailing in the wind. I move away from my life this fast. I put my *RBC Dominion Securities Portfolio Strategy Quarterly* back in my bag, not to be opened during my entire trip. These things we do by habit, like standing with one foot behind the other and leaning against a tree.

And the lodge, built of stripped yellow logs, resting on an arm of land that meets the morning sun risen from the largest natural lake in the province. At dinner I am introduced to Anna, beside me, from North Dakota. "You didn't have electricity in the '6os?"

"No, isn't that something, but we didn't seem to care."

"And no water?"

"Yes, it was cold outside in the winter."

And the difficulty of responding to someone who comes so freely out of herself that it takes my breath away. And not in any way other than in friendly terms, where the best of one person reaches out and touches the best of another.

"Did you have saskatoons?"

"We called them currants."

"Buffalo beans, brown-eyed susans, shooting stars?"

"All of those."

And such a pleasant conversation between those who come from flat land, where what you know is limitless. One horizon of land and one larger horizon of sky.

"And blue, too."

"Victoria's too rainy for me ... 30 years on."

Later, one moment I watch the lake reflect peace on the ceiling and the next, sudden drowning sleep. I hear a 6:00 AM voice under my room, on the deck where the hum of the hot tub has kept itself company through the night.

I am fed and I am taken by a vessel down the water, where a lake becomes a river and with gravity, friction and inertia flows the way of all of them: to the sea. I pass the sparse pine forest, the veins of root-tracery on the skin of the forest floor. Redfern River rapids. From above, a kind of speeding up where water gives itself to gravity and falls where the will of that other wishes. And water in its unsentient existence moves in straight lines until it contacts itself and rocks. The river becomes a spun white passage into the great pool. I had forgotten fish so far from humans they live in numbers we cannot count.

How often have I felt the weight of water on my body, the bulge above where it presses and below the twist of itself, the colour it returns where it is deepest, and the tan of the tailout below the falls. In this shallow eye I see before me 25 whitefish. Then another 25. And another 6 schools of 25. Then 5-pound rainbows in every slot. Then rainbow trout in every riffle and inside bend, each glide, each stream entrance. Those from the glacial silty waters are watery blue, larger eyed.

A table and chairs sit on the shore. We have come with hampers and a pontoon boat and a jetskiff from Tetachuck Lake to ferry us across. Peter, with moustache and teeth set across one another, with the silver bit in his eye brighter than mine or most of the others, tells us of a former life as an innkeeper. His local aboriginal friend called him "inky-bear" and did not know Peter could not understand him until he stopped at the store and talked to the manager, calling him "stroky bear." "And ah," Peter says, "he meant inn keeper and store keeper."

Through ham, tuna and cheese sandwiches and haze of beer, I hear a voice. It is the voice that always calls to me. It calls me least when I spend the day before my electronic mind, fingers typing their mistake-filled 90 words a minute, perhaps the only useful thing I learned in high school: how to type. It calls me most when it is near me. It is the voice of water.

Peter says, "And the guy had George sign something. George said, 'Let me try your glasses' and put his mark to the paper. After, he put the glasses in his breast pocket and when the manager asked him for them back, he said, 'You are such a great man I think you give the glasses to me. And I will keep them for you. Who knows — someday, I may need them, if I ever learn to read.'"

The dry irony that is Indian humour. And if you use your hands in talking and smile all the time, they trust you better than a rock. I am standing on a rock, with the slight rhythm of 4-weight and Elk Hair Caddis fly. I am drawn from people, a loner like a metronome, unclear of where I should be. The only ones I ever got to know were my children in the eight years I spent at home with them. You give yourself up to your children, knowing it is right. Then the bond was broken, and a decade has gone by. What more can I say?

The Beaver lifts me out of next day's dawn and places me on a lake no one else may have fished this year. The trail in the yielding grass results from restlessness of bears, different hour to different hour in their anonymous lives. Perhaps we as humans think our lives are more. I wonder whether that is because we can speak with complex symbols to one another and the languages of animals, most animals, cannot struggle up to the words formed by a cerebrum flowered into our skull to protect us from losing our instincts in the rush to thinking.

The diesel cough comes to rest and the pontoon nudges the shore. A knee-deep outlet river with a thousand rainbows squirting from the surface. One might think this a dream of possibility. A dream that every fisherman wishes would draw his dry fly, his Parachute Adams, Elk Hair Caddis, into a diminutive explosion. Then the tension when it is not sure the fish will come to hand. Finally, slipping the point from the scissors of the jaw and the thankful release. Reaching in is what fishing is about. The magician's trick comes to any ordinary human being if only he or she is willing to stare long enough into ribbony streams of water. This is not a dream and these are not closed eyes. This is a river so far away it does not have a name. This is the land of mirrors and the float planes that drop into them.

So frequently, so every cast, connection with a rainbow. I do not count unless I see the fly explode. I am enjoying the fine conjunction of flyline and rod and leader so that, drawn back to form a belly and then timing the leader to kiss the water, the forward stroke and haul lifts flyline and leader and fly to unfurl itself

70 feet like the wild fiddlehead in the jungle that is second-growth rain forest on the coast. In the small drop, comes to rest the fly.

Then past the necessary counting and feeling for the fish. Too-willing takers in the small feast before ice five feet thick. I snap off the gap and point and enjoy the suppleness that is a 4-weight and lime-green line, performing a circle of casts in the way beautiful girls let down their arms. Circle C from the lake into the shallows on the shore side of me, a belly formed and forward, on the touch, a single Spey or roll cast. When it has extended itself, the small circle to the small snap to 1:00 and 1:00 PM. When the belly, perhaps with a dagger point, sets itself in the air, forward into the lake the sinuous snake roll. And going around and around for hours, pleasure in the strokes. A triangle of casts comprising 360 degrees. I am transformed, a feckless boy with a straw hat, the kind of farmers in France, the kind of Cézanne in the Paris of his impression.

Then a quiet voice reaches in for me. Come back from the water. Come back from the fish. They'll be there tomorrow. When we return, we do so with hushed voices. Those who can't help keeping score return to the table, like me, unable to release the number caught. Evening is a star in our glasses. Evening is Redfern's quiet point of land. I will be the boy who looked forward and could not see where he would end up. Only I can see where I was. And in looking into those water eyes I see out the eyes I would see in.

And the heady hours of morning next, the sea-lion choke of the Beaver throttling back its rear end into the water. The pontoon skids the float. I have been where I have always been, deep within a river, its hand upon my thigh. The shaking plane, and the green foam earplugs I put in to keep its danger from me. We pull from the land of mirrors and it comes to me: here is where I have always been, here is where I am. In leaving for Victoria, I am leaving my life behind.

Animals that Go Bump
in the Day

Casting through the years leading up to me, I find memories of Rocky Mountains and lakes so robin's-egg blue they seem unreal. *Circa* 1972, I stand before a corrugated, forest green tube for catching bears prior to helicopter resettlement far from Sunwapta Lodge on the Banff–Jasper Highway. This is the country of my youth. A friend and I buy a yellow canoe and we carry it and paddle it across lakes with ice floes still setting out for different shores and down the blue cold rivers. I put out my hand to ask why thumb-thick bars are bent and a skull the size of a basketball hits so hard that had they not been there, the grizzly would have run right through me. No time to react and no time to move.

Move me 30 years forward and set me in another forest, with ferns like plumes of vegetative peacocks and the smell of death that means salmon returned for their short shrill dance. These are rivers where the fish lie on the gravel, eyes pecked out by seagulls so satiated all they do is call all day, the racket of the Killing Fields of any coastal flow.

Set me walking the gravel of a river I have never seen before, fly rod over my shoulder. Overhead the white corona of sundog surrounds the sun. In the wind-worried heads of cedar, the small-child cry of eagles. So specific are they that over the years I come to realize they land only on one branch of one tree on one stretch of river and survey the water for food. If the winter brings that tree down in a whump, smashing all the way across into the forest on the other side, the eagle will not sit on this stretch of salmon abundance for years.

Below my eyes a small, discrete, red pile. Bending over, I find it filled with ... yes, that's it, the seeds of strawberries, as though a tin of jam has been spooned onto wilderness. And then, among the instant willows that claim any new patch of gravel and send their leaves silver with the wind of afternoon, another pile of bright red jam. And then I turn to find only bush staring back at me, implacable, silent save the sound of grouse filling up my breath with fibrillating drum.

Barelegged, I wade a river that has not felt me before. It takes first my calves, my thighs and then a chill where I am a man. The bottom drops away, so I am half wading half swimming, rod in one hand, 20-pound pack on my back. My toes come back to gravel, then to gravel flanks in shallow warm water, to caddis fly larvae clinging to their horizontal world in a wind of water, the punctuation of a slipshod language. The long flats of Red Rock Run. I look up and I look down. Chum in their tens of thousands will line up like brown arrows. When they do this, they will show me that to catch them, I must run my lure among them on the bottom.

And then the pleasure of casting the fly with a live line; an oval cast, tip swung wide like the hem of a dancing skirt, and lifted high, then forward, with a haul at the end of the stroke. The black Doc Spratley crosses the green and lands in the soft water beyond. I swish my hat at the bzzz around my head. Blood appears under my watch strap, under the opposite sleeve and under my hair at the back. No wonder they call these little Stinkerbells no-see-ums. I can swat around with my hat as much as I want and never connect with these too-small creatures. They materialize from the air itself when humidity rises, at dark, all night long in the mist that lifts without fail and in the mornings when the sun has yet to invade the spaces between trees.

I swat around to surprise: a trail pressed into the tan river algae, as though a football team has lumbered downstream. The trail ends yards behind me and wetness stains the sand as tracks the size of horses' lead from the water.

I did not hear these harbingers of bugs, elk in their voluptuous, eight-foot-antler maleness. So I turn every few minutes to check my back, while the fluorescent line chooses its arc and the fly swings downstream, carrying my hopes that in time a fish may rise confidently. The Klanawa, the Cluxewe, the San Juan. Choose any river you want. In deepest rut of summer, a river carries on in endless conversation with itself, unaware of the consciousness around and in it.

Below me a sun-whitened Douglas-fir lies on broken branches where the winter river left it. In flood the tree was undercut and in the swing of indifferent water, its crown moved down the bank, cutting off a dozen foot-thick alders. Now stranded by the lower fluid of summer, its stump rises two feet above my head. I pull through broken hands and severed limbs until I stand on top.

The root ball is a snake-head Medusa. On the other side, I look into water so clear a quarter could be seen on the bottom, its numbers and the queen. In the tailout among the river stones a cutthroat trout, coloured so like them it can be seen only when it moves. Red, fan-shaped gills pass life through the insouciant pleasure of knowing it is beautiful.

I scan the broad grey gravel wash. Willows defer to the afternoon wind ... nothing. There is nothing but the feeling of eyes and the urge to drop my pack and run all the way back to my car. This is a feeling I have since come to know intimately, the feeling of being watched, a sensation seldom felt in the city phase of our lives, an antediluvian sixth sense for being a carnivore's prey. By the time you see a cougar, it's already too late. Or so they say, and I have never seen one, taking a neck in two bounds from cover.

Chest deep among the swirls of cloth that is summer water. The confident stop of a coastal cutthroat trout. The throat-slashed beauty and black speckled vest buttons hang in the air on a filament fine as a baby's hair. As mentioned, the arc from rod tip to fish mouth is purity. It is the moment when most easily the trout may be lost and so the largest thrill in all of fishing.

Later, hands of sun press sweat down my forehead, through unshaven stubble. I grab a topsy, 20-foot, 3-inch alder butt and haul myself up the bank, feet first. A simple snap and I am launched head first among the sweeping branches. It is later that I see the bruises on my shoulder, my hip. It is uncommonly good fortune, there having been a rock just below the surface. Had it not been there to stop my packsack I would have disappeared beneath the sweepers and not come back. As it is, I shake my head at the odd luck that has let me stand, wet only from head to waist.

Rod on my shoulder, I walk into my shadow like some Huckleberry Finn within a grown man's body; I have reached that stage of my life when the body and the mind begin to slide toward conclusion. My eyes no longer see the eye of a size 8 hook. I can tie an Improved Clinch Knot only because I have tied one a million times. Or I must remove my glasses and bring the eye within a few inches of one of mine. *Progressive* lenses. A word coined to make descent sound good. Yet out here with no one, with water and fish, is the only time I know my purpose. And it took 45 years to learn doing Dennis, far from clock and work. I have always felt money meant nothing, though my background is upper inclined. I have never wanted more. When it is offered I am grateful, though it does not make me spend my years in its pursuit. That I reserve for fish, and trudge back to a car like all the others in the bush; they've seen their better years long ago.

Up in the forest I swing a leg over a log and my foot comes down in the middle of a 20-pound chum with its macabre flesh of green and grey and yellow fungus. My foot passes right through to the other side. This fish didn't shoulder itself into the hushing trees, but here it rots, its white pudding flesh and intelligence that maggots become. The eyeless carcass waits patiently, milt and egg purpose completed. Here and there I see other carcasses, bellies ripped out, or only the muscle behind the head.

To my right a snap, one larger than a bird, a mink or raccoon. Then a restiveness in front. Stretching sideways around massed vegetation, my eyes pass up a neighbouring tree until revealed is a bear hardly larger than a cat.

From the brush the piercing sound of a mother I cannot see. I have heard the challenging "Hungh, hungh" of bear many times, but backed against the bank, the river's fretwork of branches below, my eyes bend away as the mother screams at me. There is no other way to put her voice than cast it in human terms: she just screams. I teeter on the brink with her enraged, individual teeth. When I take a tentative step, she charges to a rod's length, snout scenting. So I stand there in the convection wind, the rest of the afternoon it seems, alders complaining like old women.

This day and every other that will follow, I wander the bush alone. There is no point in worrying until presented with terror. I carry a trusty tin whistle, a bear banger with its shotgun blast, bear spray and air bombs to back up the banger. I can hairs-on-my-back appreciate the soft beauty of the little scoopings of jam dotting the forest. They indicate accurate nostrils and prehensile snouts picking berry after berry, then passing them through their bodies for the benefit of those who come to their homes.

A Steelhead Swims Through It

*In our family there was no clear line between
religion and fly fishing.*

— Norman MacLean,
A River Runs Through It

So begins Norman MacLean's indelible tale of pain
and beauty among the Montana mountains that
harboured a population of black-spotted westslope
cutthroat trout which would later become famous
among dry-fly purists from around the world.

Over the decades, I have returned to this
movie of Presbyterian moral dictum and memories
of green-leaved liquid that breathed significance
into my sunburned teenaged years. In my own
life there was no clear line between the morning
sun and fishing. I was lucky enough to live
upon a cliff where prairie falcons voiced their
complaint at my slip-sliding passage into
the valley below where, among boxcar-sized
blocks of prairie sandstone, lay the silver
bullets of morning.

As it ought to be, I remember the sun flooding the waiting valley and coating my filament with gold. In windows of pocket water, trout hung suspended. How simple the riches of our youth and how we took them for granted. I cast mosquito and Royal Coachman with my $12 Kmart no-name special, earned from selling golf balls in the grasshopper sun of those blue sky summers when the glorious ruins of nature were laid out beneath me. My creek south of Calgary bore a suitable name: Fish Creek.

In the intervening years, my life, like every life, turned the way water does around a rock. The years carried me to places I would not have been able to imagine — to a marriage and two daughters; through three university degrees I never really meant to enter or complete; to the surprise of turning out a poet; and then the detour of divorce — a land I hope never to revisit again.

Now, on most days, I sit in front of my computer until noon. When the sun passes into afternoon, I retire, not because I have been up since the black hours, but because I have been up too long. Nature threw me a twist some years ago and handed me a finite quantity of what I had, to that point, considered inexhaustible: health. In all its caprice it awarded me chronic fatigue syndrome, as well as the small mercy of appreciating, in its decline, that which is most precious.

And so, when I met Morgan McLean (no relation to Norman), as handsome and fine-mannered a young man as any parent could hope to have the fortune to shape into adulthood, who has fly-fished since he was a child in Ontario, it was hard to resist being charmed. And, of course, I didn't wish to.

I couldn't help but recall the other MacLean suggesting about his minister father, "To him all good things, trout as well as eternal salvation, come by grace and grace comes by art and art does not come easy."

When I suggest this to Morgan he gives, emphasizing the second syllable, a thoughtful "Mm-huh."

Fly fishing, as I have come to know it, is not really a form of fishing at all. It is an art, and its practitioners must be prepared to spend years accumulating a fine sort of knowledge, the sort that I, as a poet in another room of my life, squeeze from memory like the gush of leaves in spring. I will stumble after the fish, for it is elusive pleasure that draws us.

On the September day we descend from the mountains of Vancouver Island for a day on the Gold River system, I wear borrowed chest waders three sizes too large. Having consumed three days of energy to arrive at this river, I slide among the rocks and stalks of sapling trees in my oversize boots to a pool within a canyon the sun does not warm more than minutes every day. The pool is of a kind only memory can create, for it is not of molten glass and it is not an amber gold. It is liquid air that one can imagine leaning into and opening lungs.

Morgan unfolds his 2-weight Loomis and, with delicacy of placement, roll casts from among the waist-high rocks and spruce into water I can see as though it were not here — eight feet deep and the subtleness of its presence. Then he points out the ghosts swaying irresolutely, bellies to the bottom. "We fish for steelies by sight. If you can see them and can't catch them, then you're doing something wrong."

Early in the season, the shifting viscosities produce transient windows, allowing the fly fisher to spot his quarry. As the anadromous summer steelhead reside in their natal rivers almost a year before spawning, they must eat. Thus a waked fly for aggressive fish is employed and the bread and butter of aquatic systems: a dry fly in caddis or mayfly pattern. When cooler water prevails, a Babine Special, General Practitioner or the gaudy but simple Popsicle is sent as a swung fly closer to the bottom.

But in the low waters of September, when the leaves turn their inevitable harvest-moon hue, even the shadow of flyline will spook a summer steelhead into disappearing like a conjuror's manipulation.

"The trick is presentation, to cast the fly above the fish," Morgan says as he points to the steelhead seemingly just out of reach. His enviably smooth movement raises the rod tip, bringing his floating line across the still pool. In the same figure-eight motion, his hand crosses his face in the half-light of the canyon then back to set the belly, and the line is rolled, hand as though striking a hammer to a nail, forward and across and down upon the water.

In the silence of cedar trees that have stood their ground against the centuries, Morgan adds a stack mend so the line curls on top of the leader, sinking the fly to the bottom. In an imitation of high-stick mymphing, excess flyline is mended just enough so the egg-sucking leech tumbles the liquid terrain of broken stone in green and red and white. Just as a natural food moves passively with the imperceptible currents, the fly takes its measured course.

I find myself holding my breath and taking photographs. The situation is so beautiful I cannot spoil it by casting where a boy and a fish in their different worlds outwit one another. Later, when the negatives are developed, I find that a summer steelhead, with its translucent pectoral fins, truly is so ghostly it fails to leave a whisper of its presence.

And still later, after watching and seeking to duplicate Morgan's fluid methods, the light and my energy begin to fade. I find myself trembling before the possibility of failing with the fish, a trait I tell myself I should not feel, having snared more fish in half my life than most are given in a full one.

"Mm-huh," Morgan repeats, his thoughts indecipherable behind his polarized sunglasses. He suggests a certain pocket water spot that has hidden the fish before. Here the stream tumbles through a riffle and two rocks stick out like knees. The water falls between in a slick wet throat and then upwells into an eye of foam. Silver falls away from the lens.

"Land the fly just where the water drops. Mend the line this way and that so the fly comes straight back to you." Morgan places the tip of his first finger and thumb together to quietly emphasize his point.

So the fly and its four-pound tippet are landed. Immediately the water turns the white flyline into a snake and I'm snapping my wrist left then right and stripping as quickly as I can. Then comes the moment I connect with a steelhead rising from its summer home.

When the fish comprehends the steel shank of subterfuge, a silver streak ends at my feet then veers down with the current around a midstream rock. The line rasps across the slate. Then a wide-angled run across the breaking liquid and with the craft of slingshots the steelhead appears once more at my feet. Then the game of chess has ended, leaving only adrenaline as evidence of its passing.

Hands in my pockets I cannot hide my disappointment. The muscles of my thighs and the predator's nimble precision no longer match those of yellow summers when I would wade to my chest and never worry about the river. My mind returns to Montana and the simple appreciation of skill so beautiful it hurts: Brad Pitt in his casual masculinity, catching the wily one and disappearing, only the tip of his rod protruding from the steep-sided river shot with pieces of sun.

"You were lucky. Most steelhead fly fishers take 100 to 200 hours to hook their first fish." This kindness I accept gratefully, stumbling my tired feet and monstrous waders over speckled granite rocks and stumps that Morgan walks as though on a fence top wide as a sidewalk.

This is when Morgan leaves me with my thoughts and the drops of sweat that line my cheeks. The creases in my face have given in to years and gravity. Crossing rocks that look broken by a giant fist to force the river where it wishes, Morgan steps from rock to rock, a fall of more than his height beneath him.

From the shade wherein I rest I hear the sound of reel responding to fish. One hundred yards away on a car-sized chunk of rock stands Morgan, hands over his head, reaching as high from the shadow as he can in a frantic kind of prayer. The image will stay with me forever.

When the Montana fish was subdued, Paul MacLean offered his wet boyish grin that softened his Most Reverend father to muse that we can love completely without complete understanding. "My brother," Norman understood, "stood before us not on a bank of the Blackfoot River but suspended above the earth, free from all its laws like a work of art."

A young man of astonishing beauty looks up at me through the lens. Older, more compromised, with children and mortgages, debts and regrets, I look back at this boy almost young enough to be my own. I am thankful for the skills of others, the lessons I have not yet learned about the racing of the heart and the silver speed that sometimes touches it. This is a bond that is not spoken. There is no need, among the fragrant spruce far from the other reality, the humdrum life that is where we mostly live. These small mementoes we carry in our minds as clear as mountain water that leaves nothing and asks nothing as it carries itself and the mind toward the sea.

And there is always going back. As we roll the green hills, I note a trout ring like a note of melody on an evening pond. Morgan only laughs — at me — for the ancient desire to stop when the day is setting, at the belief the trout I have not yet caught may come. "Mm-huh," I find myself agreeing, having assumed the assurance of the young. The wheels press through the mountains.

And the last word? The last word I leave to Norman MacLean. Now an old man, he stands before his river, having lost his wild and beautiful brother and his shadow casting that made the trout leap from its home and catch the fly before it could settle, having lost his mother and his father and also his girlish wife:

"Of course I am too old to be much of a fisherman now and I usually fish the big water alone, although some friends think I shouldn't ... but when I am alone in the half light of the canyon all existence seems to fade to a being with my soul and memories and sounds of the big Blackfoot River and a four-count rhythm and the hope that a fish will rise."

Me and Bobby McGee

I look out the apartment window of the Kootenay Trout Hatchery into a black made more unfamiliar by my having driven 12 hours the afternoon before. Down Highway 93 into a terrific lightning storm where not a soul but shafts of white strode the yellow valleys, my car traversed the lonely miles with rain my constant companion.

At this early hour I should be asleep, but the rain, in its non-stop, non-corporeal language, has roused me. It falls like hail into the "moat" that surrounds the compound. It is the westslope cutthroat trout that have me up in the dark. Even though my eyes swim through weariness, the date with the fish won't let me sleep. Upon the venetian blinds are projected the wavering wrinkles of water like some odd Broadway sign blinking its middle-of-the-night neon message of isolation.

The shadows on the water slip here and there with the slowly roiling water. They arc and converge and I wipe sleep from my eyes. Now I understand that I am looking directly down onto some of the largest Girard rainbow trout I have ever seen, plying their night world, without the need of sleep.

In the darkened apartment with the shadow of fish streaming the walls like living wallpaper, I hold my breath and gather my stuff: 6-weight rod, 4.5-pound tippet, raincoat, clippers and all the etceteras. Gerry will bring the flies. After I've eaten my Cheerios and drunk my Tetley tea, his truck slithers to a halt on the wet asphalt. I hoist my packsack of camera gear, lunch and essentials, fearing I will hear what I do not wish to know: that the rain has loosened the clay and the Wigwam River is blown.

I am not much more comforted as we press down the old Fort Steele highway, passing thunka-thunk over the Bull River bridge; the water below is a lazy brown serpent where nary a westslope cutthroat trout could see a 5/0-sized grasshopper if it glowed in the dark. But, sitting in the back with rods and reels and the flotsam that is fly fishing, and rocking with sleepy highway motion and the warm, moist heat demisting the windows, I keep my counsel to myself.

In the front, Gerry and Tom and Barry sing along, thumping the dashboard in time to Janis Joplin's version of the old Kris Kristofferson song. "Windshield wipers slappin' time I's holding Bobby's hand in mine, We sung every song that driver knew." Janis belts out her cigarette-raspy, Southern Comforted blues voice that arrived from another planet during what now seem the gentle, sophomoric, amber-coated '60s.

The windshield wipers are indeed slapping down with a volume of water that matches Niagara Falls and the wet, summer-yellowed fields and their dottings of lodgepole pine slide by. Turning right at Elko onto the mountain gravel road we leave the highway and its wet transit to Kalispell, Montana.

My disappointment arises from expectation. Prior to pushing the pedal to the floor in a one-white-Subaru caravan heading east I had done my research. The Cranbrook area is home to North America's best bet for the finely dappled, yellow-flanked westslope cutthroat trout.

After a damaging flood in the early 1980s, the then Ministry of Fisheries instituted what was at the time a novel, ingenious management regime to bring back the area's 18 rivers. By closing certain sections of the now justly famous Elk, St. Mary, Bull, Skookumchuck and Wigwam rivers, by introducing strict limits, catch-and-release zones and fly fishing-only zones, the ministry's plan has resulted in the fishery's rebounding to the point of surpassing the fabled waters of Montana and Idaho to the south, made famous in Robert Redford's paean to religion and fly fishing, *A River Runs Through It*.

Today, this tiny portion of the Columbia drainage system is home to the finest Westslope cutt fishing in the world, a fishery that every year makes top-ten lists in magazines from New York City to Sydney, Australia. An honest 20- to 40-fish day for adept fly fishers.

So famous are these waters that Barry Alexander in the front seat, a sod lucky enough to make your teeth splinter in jealousy, laconically tells the windshield, "I flew in from Kenai, Alaska, yesterday."

"Yeah?" Gerry smoothes his broad moustache down the sides of his face. Quietly I contemplate the red tinge inside my eyelids as Barry matter of factly says he wanted to try the king on the fly as well as the sockeye. He is quietly scornful of the sockeye fishery which, due to high fish numbers and the meat-hunting attitude of participants, is, to his mind, essentially a snag fishery. Barry goes on to casually relate that he fishes 200 days a year around the world from a base in Australia. Though he doesn't indicate the source of funding for his prodigious habit, he does add that he buys all his gear in Singapore — because it's cheaper. And he's here "because this one's special."

We rise around foothills that break into rock above us, the tectonically shoved-together fabric of the Purcell Mountain Range, and begin the caterpillar crawl up the well-washed gravel road with its tossings of rain-loosened rock sprinkled here and there. We crunch to a halt at mile 41, almost into Montana, where the Wigwam rises before cascading from the mountains to the Elk

River flats and Lake Koocanusa, the reservoir for the Kootenay River that extends once again south into Idaho and Montana.

It turns out that Barry has also done his homework, over the Internet from Australia. "These rivers are so untouched and so cold that cutts are the dominant trout, holding this niche that rainbow can't enter easily. This is one of the few areas in the world where local westslopes remain pure, unhybridized with rainbows — as has happened so often in warmer waters to the south."

"Wait until you see the colour. They have a golden glow that seems to gleam right out of the fish," Gerry proffers and bumps us down a long steep spline into the Wigwam valley. We crunch down through puddles and willow that bend from the bumpers onto a small ledge by a river. I am surprised to find the river is as blue and clear after a 24-hour deluge as though the rain itself has cleaned and deepened the hue.

This is a high mountain stream typical of the Rockies, so high it's liquid glass and layers of air tumbling across broken mountain stone that lift almost three-D from their riverbed home. Certainly the river looks too high in the mountains to support much in the way of chironomids and mayflies.

As if noting my dubious, scrutinizing eyes, Gerry points to a small cutback where the channel has changed its freestone path this spring. "Three cutts in that small eddy."

"It's hardly 10 feet across," I say in disbelief. Gerry shrugs and Barry, putting on his small magnifying specs and a size 18 mosquito, points at first one rise and then another. The dry fly fluff is landed and disappears just as quickly.

"Ah, cutthroat trout. A guide's best friend," Gerry beams as the rest of us rig up. He might as well be hooking his thumbs behind some large red suspenders and holding forth in a rural, straw-between-the-teeth superiority. As it is, he stands, impervious to the rain, in his bomber jacket, shorts and river boots.

Releasing them in short order, as though waiting for my camera were an indignity for a beautiful fish, Barry proceeds, methodically, to place his mosquito in front of the second riser, take that and then the third. This in water I had disdained as being sterile of insects and of fish.

The rain keeps falling and coating everything with liquid colour. Soon I am wading the bluer-than-blue river, its lens bulging against my leg. Then I land up to my armpits, whacking my tailbone on a rock. With my neoprene legs refusing to get beneath me, this distant river of a distant mountain land swirls me to the edge of a pool, where my hand secures a rock before I am sucked into the beauty of manless wilderness.

Miraculously, my camera in my chest pocket is dry and, other than my arms to my armpits, so am I. Willows droop lugubriously from the bank as I stroke and stroke the caddis fly to the fast-moving slate-wall side where, from the drifting windows, the small bullet of yellow-silver becomes one with the line that touches the first finger on my left hand. The flanks with their generous dappling of fine brown spots and a yellow that truly glows with a tinge of blue in this blue-cold water are admired. Released, the fish snaps back into its alien, soundless world.

At my feet, I discern what I have taken to be a puff of clay. It turns before my eyes into a white line that rises from the deep and wavers closer and closer to my boots. My second thought is — how the mind plays tricks — that it is an electric cord shimmering and connected. Then the water throws the image clear and true: flyline. Pulling on it hand over hand I soon have a complete flyline in my hand, and now backing. From the depths a reel bumps toward my feet. Almost my first catch of the day: a Cabelas reel, fully loaded and possibly dropped in the same way that I lost my footing.

With my wet hands, with my rod under my arm in rain that will not cease pouring off spruce and rock, off hat brim and nose, that insinuates itself, it seems, even within the air, I reel and watch the fast water where cutthroat rise for insects I cannot see.

Then the visual gift of a well-stuffed box of flies. This is one of the pleasures of the fly fisher: to look with anticipation and appreciation into the box of another man's skill: rubber-legged grasshopper, Elk Hair Caddis, the mysterious Madame X, bead head Pheasant Tail, pale evening Dun and "floating" nymph.

Gerry, who has been standing with his hands in the pockets of his shorts, says, "Cutts like flies high and dry. Elk and deer hair should be harvested in the fall and winter when it's thick and fat and hollow."

"Sheer beauty if you ask me."

Then a boom that takes hold of our lungs and squeezes before echoing down the valley off the bluffs of rock. Our eyes jerk upstream and Gerry chomps down on his soggy cigarette so it resembles a bent, winter finger. "Looks like we have company. That was a bear banger."

We hold each other's shoulders and make our way across the river, sweep through willows that recede from our passage. Upstream, we meet up with the others at a pool so blue it is green. At the top end, a riffle plunges from its own insides and all of us gather at the long deep run. The tailout rises toward us as though trying to communicate something perfectly clear but in a language known only to itself.

Once again, Barry points to the cutback at the top and lands his offering in the foam. Releasing that piece of jewellery, he then points to another trout sipping the far shore. "That man's a hunter of fish," Gerry confides to me. Rain running freely off my nose, shivering and feeling unfishy, I find this completely convincing.

The small race disappears into blue at every angle, the way headlights careen off mountain walls. At least a dozen cutts are secreted. I find myself just watching Barry, who has, I notice, small growths on the side of his cheek, a flushing of them as though a herd of diminutive buffalo roam the plains of his face searching for a way to break through. Is it Hodgkin's? Melanoma? How long does this man have?

First with a mended, dead-drifted fly, then with a skated fly, he takes one fish after another off to the side, without disturbing the others beneath its surface. Finally he stands in the tailout, casting directly upstream for a fussy cutt that shoulders through the stained glass the river gives up to us, browned by the blue and persistent rain that coats the forest with perception.

Barry mends directly back to himself, and the cutt launches itself with a fly in the scissors of its mouth. And then the fine taper, the nail knot and whiteness of flyline leave the water. For a moment, like Brad Pitt in the scene where sun paints gold on his shadow-cast streamer decades ago in the Blackfoot River, from shaken mouth to fly rod tip the long moment suspends in our eyes.

Later, by the truck, branches are broken over knees, twigs are harvested from beneath the shaggy arms of spruce. The smoke makes its own white language in the trees. As so often happens at the end of the day, I am left with nothing but a hoagie in my teeth, and that indefinable presence of where we live and fish out our days. We do this because we need offer no reason for its necessity, because, in their coming and going, these are the few days for which we are truly alive — days of blue and oranges, of succulent water that requires no justification, no need of cellphones or laptops, no reminders of responsibilities that wait.

And then the rods are broken down, the floatant and snippers and hemostats taken off our necks. The windshield wipers are slapping down again. We are silent, driving down the day. And just as nonchalantly miraculous, Kris Kristofferson offers his own pre-alcohol version of hitting the road, pulling his "harpoon out of my dirty red bandana," Bobby — his Bobby being a woman — and the genderless love from the '60s when we were young.

The last thought I grant to the Girards at the hatchery. Rainbows as thick as your arm, painted red down their flanks, have not spoken a word all day, have not moved anywhere but through their captive world within a moat around my room. We all stop and bend our heads, thinking the same thought: "Too bad you can't fly-fish at a hatchery."

Rainbows Land in Columbia Country

Credited with being the first white man to explore the Castlegar area, David Thompson arrived in 1807, some years before Franklin's ill-fated expedition found itself wasting away in a vain quest to map the shores of the Arctic Ocean. What Thompson found was not so forbidding. As he rolled up his sleeves on the warm, arid, southern valley his eyes beheld the confluence of the Columbia and Kootenay rivers.

So large are the rivers that today the Hugh Keenleyside Dam to the north of town controls 8.8 trillion cubic metres of live Columbia storage while the Brilliant Dam to the east controls only slightly less of Kootenay waters. Combined flow averages about 60,000 cubic feet per second on the 26-mile trip to the American border at Waneta.

Commerce was quick to follow Thompson's route. By 1887 the Canadian Pacific Railway had completed the rail link in the area, and paddle-wheelers, including the *Minto*, carried goods down the fast-flowing river. Lead and zinc ore was barged across the river. The train station, a replica of the 1906 wood structure that burned to the ground, stands today as a museum.

At about the time the rail station lit the night sky, the most interesting Castlegar residents, the Doukhobors, arrived to establish an agrarian society — actually 23 in western Canada — while escaping religious persecution from the Russian Orthodox Church. Termed "spirit wrestlers," sect members based their beliefs on recognizing God and loving their neighbours as themselves. This led to their famous stand under leader Peter Verigin, whose tomb is a local attraction, against militarism and all forms of violence.

Today, the river in all its breadth and power slips through Castlegar in the same gorge where pioneers first viewed its half-mile blue width. Arriving in my Subaru station wagon on the 400-mile mountain drive from Victoria almost a hundred years later, I spill over the same ridge and down to the coiling blue serpent that is the Columbia. Stopping my car along the ridge, I can sense the river's great power, its voice rising with the dry heat like the sound of distant trains.

The reason for my trek is not religious in a Judeo-Christian sense, but follows a purpose mysteriously persuasive nonetheless. I have a date with Columbia rainbow trout, rumoured to fatten in this huge environment to fabled 5- and even 10-pound fish. As if to prove the allegation, while local guide Dwayne D'Andrea and I slide the drift boat off the trailer, a sturgeon lifts its 8-foot, 300-pound bulk a clear 8 feet from the water where the rivers join and smacks down like a log.

Soon, like a millennium version of Huck Finn and Tom Sawyer, our boat is swung within the grasp of the great river and swirled away as though it were a chip of bark. The sound of the river is all that can be heard as it piles against the pylons of the Highway 3 bridge, pushing up a six-foot lip of water against the concrete abutments.

Instantly I comprehend that this is no ordinary river. As I look across a half mile of swiftness, two questions formulate themselves clearly in my mind: where do the rainbows lie in water that may reach 120 feet deep; and just how impossible would it be to try and anchor in such a massive flow?

"Consider this a river-within-rivers fishery," Dwayne offers, pointing to little nooks and crannies where back eddies swirl from behind rock projections along the shore. Surprisingly, or at least I am surprised to learn this, the warm summer afternoons and evenings produce massive caddis fly hatches. Hence in all this water, a dry fly out-produces all other offerings. Out comes my 5-weight rod with its green floating line. A 10-foot leader of 3.8-pound-test monofilament nail knots its connection to the floater. A yellow-bodied humpie graces the tip of one leader, a grasshopper the other.

The shadows of afternoon climb down the western shore and begin reaching out into the river. As shade provides more cover and hence improves the confidence of the native rainbow, we fish hard to the shore. It is also cooler here, prompting the emergence of moisture- and temperature-sensitive insects.

A few false casts later, my fly sits for a second near the small dimple of a hesitant trout. I find it remarkable that in a river 800 yards wide and flowing like a herd of semi-trailers, small shore pockets billow up their fluid much like the pocket water of a small stream. And then my fly is waking across the surface, and I wait. The trout will not come to me but to Dwayne, who soon releases a sparkling pink- and brown-spotted rainbow beside the boat.

A few casts later I am still unsuccessful. Behind and in front of the boat, trout rise with speckled regularity, moving with the rising water and keying in on insects that I cannot see. I hold forth that the size of my fly might be downgraded. The answer is another take of a 15-inch trout — for Dwayne. Now, I am not normally a competitive spirit, but there is something rather primal (nothing to do with testosterone, I'm sure) that irks my male ego when it's out-fished. This is true even when I calmly reason that the answer is quite simple: a local angler should always out-fish the newcomer because of the latter's insubstantial knowledge. That being ciphered doesn't make it easier to swallow, however — by me at least.

Long years of fishing have taught me that ego needs to be submerged to improve success. I cast a baleful, scrutinizing eye at the fly that lands delicately among the small upwellings. They dapple the surface like irregular eyes of magnifying glasses, as though if only one were to look close enough, one could see down their lenses all the way to China.

What I see is a deer hair grasshopper sitting high and dry. Then it is lifted and double-hauled to some eight feet in front of a swirl. And then nothing. "Well, this is early, the big boys haven't arrived yet," says Dwayne and sets his rod down for the pull back out into the main current.

Down the spruce and yellow-leaved-poplar banks the drift boat turns. We are alone with the large grandness of river and stump of tree, as the boat circles so small as to be a non-existent smudge on nature, perhaps a small cloud that forms over a mountain and melts away in its rush to the next valley bottom. Again a sturgeon erupts from the water, prehistoric and eerie, to emphasize humanity's short tenure in this landscape.

I take a moment to inspect my reel. One hundred fifty yards of 20-pound Dacron backing indicates the reality of large fish and strong current. On smaller reels, Spiderwire proves necessary due to its thinner diameter. The downside of this approach is that it can cut the fingers as the fish slices into the depths of the Columbia. Getting the fish on the reel so the drag system can perform its purpose appears the proper option.

The bow of the boat edges into the paler, gentler light of evening settling upon the Bar D Bar pool. Calling the waters a pool does little to indicate the challenge faced by the angler. At this point the rocky shores on both sides of the Columbia divert its course, resulting, on the western shore, in a 90-foot-deep back eddy approximately 500 yards long. The rock along the eastern shore turns that part of the current out into the main channel, producing an enormous back eddy absolutely in the centre of the river.

The mid-river back eddy powers so strongly that complete tree stumps travel a half mile below us, then turn and ride the current all the way back up, almost to our boat, and then swing around the whirling edge and follow the water back down again. The size of the Columbia cannot be conveyed adequately on paper other than to compare it with the pull and rough freedom of the ocean.

Now the humidity is rising. Now the temperature floats in the free fall of its early evening apogee. Along the steep shoreline dotted with pines comes the largest black bear I have ever seen.

"I'm sure glad I'm in this boat," I say, knowing that there must be 50 feet of water beneath us.

"Don't be too sure," Dwayne counters. "Sometimes the bears can smell the restaurant across the river and simply wade in and swim."

"Hmm," I say, feeling not quite so safe. I can imagine a bear slipping in for a dip and being carried literally miles before reaching the other side, and then resolutely beginning the upstream trek toward what smelled like an easy and filling meal.

And now the caddis flies begin their upward flight, diminutive angels appearing from nowhere. The river sends its billowing arms toward the shore, and then another successive upwelling boils from closer in. And where they meet is a short exchange of pushing until the stronger prevails. It dawns on me what Dwayne refers to as a "river-within-rivers" fishery. The insects that comprise the rainbows' diet slide across the surface like crumbs upon a linoleum floor. The water in its many curlings is a broom that sweeps the surface, collecting insects in its crease first to one side and then, as that pocket of current spends itself, turning and sweeping from another direction.

In other words, my technique has been incorrect. Although I have caught a number of smaller, less discriminating rainbows, my waked fly, sending off its V of water, has simply moved the fish away. These fish are looking for passively floating, i.e., dead-drifted insects and my fly must imitate this natural pattern. I cast into the seam of water and when it moves away from the boat, feed line into it. When, on the other hand, the seam and boat come closer, the line needs mending. A quick snap of the fly upon which my eyes have rested provides assurance of my amended technique.

I look down and find my legs crawling with caddis. A hatch as thick as fur catches fire in the blue. My bare arms become forests for antennae-twitching bugs. From the rim of my hat, chains of insects much like bees from a beekeeper drip. And all around us the languid rises, the leaps of trout among the seams.

Similarly anointed with emergent ones, Dwayne suggests, "Sometimes the hatch is so strong it's a lottery that they'll even see your fly. In these cases the philosophy of going against the hatch is the only possibility."

With insects flowing from my face and dark descending like a slow mouth, my eyes have lost the ability to distinguish my own synthetic food way out there beyond my green streamer. Of course, it would be this time that the true hard pull of a large trout speeds into the territory of the unseen, jolting me from reverie.

And then the rising of the tip that indicates a turned and determined animal speeding directly at the boat. I lift the rod high and reel far behind my head while trying to back up over seats and life jackets and tackle boxes. I catch up just as the fish comes under the bow and then the rod tip goes from 16 feet in the air to 3 feet under the water. And then the battle, as abruptly as it began, is over.

In darkness, Dwayne rows the long pull to the far shore. I am in the bow, silent with the unfilled promise of a rainbow. From the dark, a whirlpool many feet deep in the centre turns lazily toward the boat. Dwayne moves by on the lip and we are spun in a circle. Definitely the Columbia favours not the novice.

At the shore we load the boat in full darkness, now lit with stars and the incessant sweet voice of cricket legs. Midges fill the backup lights and we catch them in our hands and mull our possibilities.

"There's always another evening," and a considering glintiness fills Dwayne's eyes. Wondering how small we can tie a midge tomorrow, I find I can access mutual agreement. What I look back on before the truck clunks into gear is history: paddlewheelers, the pacific Doukhobors, and Thompson's frail and small canoes. The blackness of the night water stretches out, now only a danger; how we fear history, accustomed as we are to the light of present day.

Seasons of the Somass

Sent from England by his doctor in 1913, Brigadier-General Noel Money brought to Canada his two-handed Wye rods. His graceful double Spey cast arced across the waters that would someday bear his name. Although he called the dropping into dark water below his cabin on the Stamp River "The Great Pool," today it is known by anglers as "Money's Pool."

At the family estate, Culmington Manor in Shropshire, the brigadier was raised on Atlantic salmon, and his stuffed, leather-bound game book recorded his days there and then his years on the Somass system. Similarly recorded is his penchant for sinking red or orange flies in high water as well as his preferred lowwater dressings, offered on the end of a floating line.

General Money fished Vancouver Island's greatest river and its prodigious flow with the young magistrate Roderick Haig-Brown, who regarded him as a mentor. Neither lived to witness the changes that time has laid upon the Somass:

the Robertson Creek hatchery and a much wider range of gear and technique, including the zoom of winter jetboats.

Since the 1970s, the Robertson Creek hatchery has become justly famous. First built to enhance pink salmon runs, the facility soon branched out into steelhead. Chinook salmon followed. And these were not just any chinook. They were — and are — the famed 20- to 40-pound Robertson Creek chinook. Although typically averaging 30,000 fish over the years, this run reached a staggering total return in 1991 of 292,335 fish. It is little wonder these chinook spawned the impressive saltwater sport fisheries that made Barkley Sound famous: the Bamfield summer fishery on the rolling surfline beauty, Cape Beale with its white beacon and apron of rock and the Port Alberni Labour Day festival.

But the Somass system has other species of equal or greater importance to sport fishermen. Originating in the large central lakes — Sproat and Great Central — the Sproat and Stamp rivers funnel Vancouver Island's greatest sockeye run from the Somass to spawning gravel along the shores and in the streams above the lakes. With an optimum escapement (the fish remaining *after* all commercial, native and sport fisheries) of 350,000 sockeye, these two rivers have felt the weight of runs as large as 1.8 million sockeye.

Stand along Money's Run, the classic 800 yards above his pool, in September when at 2:00 PM the sun illuminates the yellowy green glass in a valley of curved and leaning Douglas-fir and you will see relentless movement as though the bottom itself is migrating upstream. The slipping shadow is sockeye beginning to change into their well-known greens and reds. These colours transmit through transient portholes as grey. A kind of vertigo it is to watch, almost spooky its relentless crawling.

Another bright spot in recent years has been an abundance of hatchery coho salmon. In 1999, for example, the Stamp River counter (located high in the system), recorded 42,583 adult fish. While this does not measure Sproat River fish, or wild coho that spawn below the hatchery (or in the Somass proper), the methodological distinction is moot — in-river retention fisheries for coho have been authorized for 1998 onward during a period when most of the rest of the province suffered coho closures.

The fecundity of the Somass system is clear. So full of life is it, with good amounts of algae supporting invertebrate and vertebrate life, in fact, that the system supports a 12-month calendar of fishing opportunities.

Not surprisingly, winter is the time of year to fish for winter steelhead. The Somass may rise as much as 10 feet and upwards of 10,000 steelhead may enter the river. Some intrepid anglers have been known to drift in at 4:30 AM and stake out the best spots of the Stamp and Sproat conjunction and await the watery dawn light that slithers over the mountains a few hours later. This Confluence Pool provides a huge, winter back eddy that forms on the south shore; this is where the steelhead lie belly to bottom.

The winter steelheaders' gear of choice is a bait-casting reel mounted on a 10.5-foot rod. Terminal tackle includes a dink float, split shot and Gooey Bobs or Jensen eggs, or roe when natural bait is allowed. For backtrollers, deepdiving hotshots or huge flatfish are lowered to the fish behind the drift boat. Colours of choice include blue, green, red, chartreuse and the Pirate combination (blue, green and red).

From time to time, jetboats disturb the treetops with their roar. Seasoned steelheaders have learned to indulge these noisy critters: the passage of a jetboat will often stir up resting steelhead, resulting in the cry of "Fish on." Two other time-tested tips include using smaller bait and hook in low, clear water and fishing closer to shore with bigger gear in high, cloudy water.

Almost as winter gives way to spring, the first sockeye salmon begin nosing up the 30-mile channel of Alberni Inlet. Like other anadromous species, sockeye enter the Somass estuary on a rising tide. The end of May brings the first of these fish two miles farther, to Paper Mill Dam.

This natural obstruction at the upper end of a huge pool was the site of an ill-fated mill established in 1891 to produce paper from recycled paper, rags and woody weeds. At the height of its activity, the mill included a boardwalk of shops and buildings that crossed the river's flow. But the venture was not successful, and today it is hard to understand why a river that could rise 10 feet would have been bridged by buildings from one side to the other. The grinding mill has long since been reabsorbed into the west coast rain forest and all that remains are a few pilings on the left side of the river that, at low water, vibrate like bows.

The remaining "waterfall" (a drop of about six feet) where the mill drew its power is the site of a sockeye fishery that should be on every angler's annual Vancouver Island freshwater calendar. Unrivalled it is for opportunity and for the sheer pandemonium of its precise fishing technique. Upwards of 12 anglers will line each side of the river, just above the falls. A dink float is placed — brace yourself — 10 to 13 feet above two ounces of pencil lead inserted into surgical tubing. A simple swivel ties on and three feet of leader ends in a 1/0 steelhead hook onto which an orange or chartreuse yarn fly is tied.

Anglers cast upstream in turn; the first, which is the angler farthest downstream, aims to extend the float, weight and fly in a straight line from the rod tip. As the first float hits the water, the next angler casts. The in-a-wave procession of rods and floats is sheer ballet to watch, but difficult to perform. Woe be he who crosses lines or casts out of turn, for he will be thrown over the waterfall by the skilled but irascible locals. During the run's peak, every angler will catch his limit.

In summers of low water, sockeye can be taken on the fly in certain stacking spots along the system. And here is something not every angler knows: no salmon eats in freshwater, and thus the reader may be left wondering, as all fishing is based on trying to get a fish to have a close encounter of the tooth kind with a lure, fly or bait, why anyone would ever catch a salmon in freshwater.

Fortunately for anglers there are half a dozen other reasons why salmon will bite when they return to freshwater. The first three are: territoriality, this is my space, you get out of it, regarding another redd-robbing salmon or egg-rustling trout; aggression, the swimming-out-of-the-pack response and whacking something out of existence; and hormonal, the I don't know why I'm doing it, I just can't help it.

At the Falls Pool on the Stamp River above the Somass one day, using a truly ugly half-blue and half-silver knubbly spoon, I landed, while most around me were skunked, 52 coho on one three-inches-of-rain day. Among those, I caught one particular 20-pound male four times. I asked it, "I can see you biting once and maybe even twice, but four times?" The fish looked me in the eye as I levered the hook from its jaw and said, "I don't know why, I just gotta have it." That's hormonal.

The fourth bite trigger is curiosity, the bite of the coho. When sight fishing, sweep your spinner in front of a coho and it will lock on sensors. It will follow within a foot of the lure for as far as 25 feet, a great distance, and that is locked-on curiosity. (When it's out of sight, you can tell a coho is following as the spinner's blade loses its drag and momentarily slips toward the rod tip. Add another split ring and a black hook to take these touchers but not biters.) Once curiosity has been satisfied, the fish begins shifting its snout back and forth. As this behaviour presents the lure to one eye and then the other, it probably represents a form of triangulation to lock on the lure. Once this head shaking begins, there is only one outcome: biting the lure. Try to contain your adrenaline until you feel the bite on the rod. I'm not good at this and tend to yank the lure out of the water to rocket past my head into the forest as the fish's mouth opens.

The next trigger is far and away the most common bite reflex of salmon: the passive bite. This occurs when stacked-together salmon, in runs and heads of pools, keeping their stations, will mouth any small piece of detritus and let it go; this includes your offering, usually a yarn fly below a float or a fly. Sockeye, chum, pink and chinook display this behaviour so strongly that it is the most important bite a fisher must learn to recognize. The float may only diddle a little or the flyline may only slow for a few seconds as the fish mouths the fluff and lets it go. Sproat River sockeye waiting at the Confluence Pool for the cover of night will mouth a small pink, orange or red fly — a Popsicle or Tequila Sunrise will suffice — in the lie just off the sandstone ledge.

The final trigger is scent. I stood squinty-eyed above the still waters of Sproat Lake where the river gathers itself to begin the downhill tumble to the Somass. Looking at a lovely mint steelhead I put a glob of roe on the spoon, the same silly knubbly one I used at the Falls Pool. I asked the fisher with me if it looked good and he only laughed. Undeterred, I chucked it out and guided it so that it would swing in front of the steelhead. Just as it moved across the steelhead, a coho rocketed out of the blue distance more than 15 feet away. Before the steelhead could respond, the coho whacked the glob. This became one of my epiphanies, a kind that all intense anglers suddenly apprehend and one that then informs their understanding of fishing for the rest of their lives. The lure had curved its passage toward the shore, letting go scent that passed down river. When it had completed its swing, the most potent shaft of scent moved back in the water. This the coho could smell even though it was completely out of sight, zero in and come to the lure unerringly.

The Somass has other fish of interest. Gorgeous, summer-run steelhead begin entering with the sockeye salmon in late May. Known as the Miracle Mile in the past, the one-and-a-half-mile stretch between Somass Park and the river's Confluence Pool gained its name from the results of an enterprising hatchery program. To prevent steelhead from dashing through the system to the Robertson Creek hatchery (and being essentially lost to anglers), staff released smolts downstream, resulting in a mile of the Somass where summer-runs still congregate for weeks before resuming their upstream trek. At any one time, as many as 1,250 of them may be in the system.

But to the fly angler, September and its low water present Money's Run at its easiest, though not its best, fishing; that occurs when another two feet of water pass down the classic run of rolled freestones in their grey, red, tan, green and brown. The Spey angler has a distinct advantage as the trees close on the waters so much that they hang out over the run, rendering a single-handed rod, with its need for back cast room, much less useful than the smooth, belled elegance of the pantheon of Spey casts. With the snake roll, the angler may cast across when upstream obstructions are behind. When they are below, on the "dangle," the angler draws a single Spey above the body and redirects the line across the current, or uses a snap T.

But in September the run is the most beautiful because it is the only time of year the angler can, in casting down the river, wade across the green bands and fish the opposite side. A lovelier steelhead run cannot be found. The angler's love of fishing is returned by the river when he or she may cross at will to present a fly more perfectly to where it has put the fish.

And of course, there is a Murphy's Law to fly fishing, and it is this: no matter which side of the river you are on, the fish are always on the other side. Money's Run is consistent with this law of nature. Money's Pool, at the bottom end of this beautiful line of great trees and slipping water, is best fished on the opposite side from where Money built his cabin on the bluff above the river. I have often wondered, in moving across the currents, how he fished this pool from the outside of its bend, as it is very hard to cast a single-handed rod, and even though a double hander will move the fly out, it will inevitably be pushed in to shore by the current and the run of shore to the right. I have been told that Money also stepped down to a lower fishing world and used a rod with a float, and this may account for success on his side of the river.

And perhaps he had a boat to carry him across, for the pool is best attacked from the inside bend on the far side under the long canopy arms of Douglas-fir. In wading out to waist level, the angler notes the bottom drop into invisibility. On Money's near side, just below the cold creek that enters, and at the pool's head, the steelhead and cutthroat trout will lie. These cutthroat are probably the wariest of the entire river, for in this spot they bite so tentatively, so short, they seldom get *pricked* by a hook, as Money himself might have observed to Haig-Brown.

It is now, in writing this, that I have discovered the way to catch these yellow trout with fine brown speckles on their bellies. One learns some simple rules that the casual observer may find pretty ho hum but to the angler, they represent lightning bolts of meaning, because they take scores of years to learn. And here is how Money's cutthroat may be caught on the fly. First, the rule: when fish bite long, fish long; when fish bite short, fish short. This occurred to me in the windy afternoon fishery of the Nitinat River one day. When fish bite long, this means they will take the fly farther down their mouth and thus you may use a highly visible fly with a long tail that extends far past the bend of the hook. As this is more easily seen by motivated fish, you will catch more (I hasten to add that when you fish small cutthroat that bite long, change the rule to fish short — for example, a Doc Spratley over a leech pattern — to avoid their sustaining gill injuries).

When fish bite short, your longer flies, the Courtney, a complex Woolly Bugger, will receive only taps on the farthest tail fibres, and you will catch no fish that day. So, move to the shorter flies, like the various Doc Spratleys, a small Muddler Minnow or nymphy-type, bead-head, gangly-legged flies that seldom extend beyond the bend, the point and the gap.

Although summer steelhead may appear in Money's Pool as early as June, the main part of the run comes this distance in early September and large numbers hold in the cold-water flume from the Ash River.

Good quantities of stragglers may be found insinuated among the coho and chinook salmon which mark the beginning of fall fishing in August.

Fall is the time of change. Nature turns itself inside out with colour and anglers match the low-angled sun with spinners, K3s and Colorado spoons. With either brass or silver spinners, these lures in red, pink, green or blue can be seen by the angler all the way through the shifting windows. As mentioned earlier, this proves disadvantageous, as the anticipating fisher watches the fish snap toward the lure and, just as the jaws open, pulls the lure out of the fish's mouth. If you suffer this all-too-common malady, fish in early morning or late evening, when low-angle light — not to mention darkness — proves too great for polarizing sunglasses to penetrate.

As the annual cycle of fishing seasons renews itself in early winter, 20,000 chum salmon rise into the Somass on a flooding tide. Few of these fish make it as far as the Stamp River counter, preferring instead to spawn in the lower reaches of the Somass. Here and on other Van Isle rivers, a yarn fly and dink float set-up fished in a typical steelhead run proves the ticket. Don't be surprised to see a diligent fly fisher plumbing the stacking fish with a chartreuse or pink fly on an intermediate sink line. Glow-in-the-dark Flashabou in orange or green provides a nicely visible fly in the low light and coming winter rain.

Even with the rain and rising water levels of winter, the Somass system remains relatively clear and fishable. Almost a century ago, General Money would poke his head from his small cabin and muse that it was a fine day to fish. With satisfaction he then hauled out, once again, the long cane rod brought from the family estate.

A new possibility, provided chinook escapements prove adequate, is a drift-boat fishery for the tidal portion of the Somass (below Paper Mill Dam). Nothing could be more suitable to a family outing and introduction to fishing than backtrolling for chinook larger than the child on the other end of the line, on a mild, broad river, ending near Clutesi Marina in the centre of town. Another new fishery to add to the Labour Day saltwater derby. Were he here today, perhaps Brigadier-General Money would approve.

Proving the Somass Sockeye

The fish swim by here. I look from my room and see them. In the greatest pool, of Stamp and of Sproat rivers. Water greens the sedimentary shelves. The indolent schools of sockeye are bars of afternoon silver.

In their season, the fish return from open ocean, reach sex and death. Pulled by genes that tell them to come, pulled by hormones that tell them to come, their return is a mystery of steering by stars, by temperature, by angle of sun and finally by scent. Once the salmon is close, once it ripens, it follows a siren's song of doing what ought to be.

These fish, with brains the size of peas, prove size means nothing to the symmetry of lives, to the purpose of all living things: to reproduce themselves. Salmon are so well guided they forage in the open ocean in the same grid mark as their parents and move back to spawn within 100 yards of where they nosed from the gravel as yellow-sacked alevins two to seven years before.

This is as it has been for more than 10,000 years. And it is an oddity, I think in the evening light that falls between fir trees and briefly on the spring-scented needles falling among them, that there were no salmon in what is now British Columbia before that time. It seems that such clarity of purpose should be proof of instinct honed longer than a flame. Consider that for the first 4 billion years of the Earth's own history there was no oxygen, there was no life. But a billion years since? That is what a salmon's instinct should be. But this is not true.

The last ice age buried Vancouver Island and the mainland of B.C. under a mile of ice. The land was pushed as much as half a mile beneath sea level and where there is no land there is no river. Thus there were no salmon. Until the ice retreated and they moved north, slowly, as strays from other rivers and became adapted to their own so that, for instance, the sockeye moving below me will, contrary to the normal habits of sockeye in other rivers, come together in the gravel beaches of the lakes above.

Another interesting tidbit about these fish that wait, piled like firewood, in the soft water of the confluence is that, also contrary to common belief, there are more of them today than time itself could stock the river with. In the 1970s, the federal government fertilized Sproat Lake with the elemental building blocks of life, including nitrogen and phosphorous. What was a run of 70,000 sockeye, even though fertilization ceased decades ago, is now, in a good year, 700,000 fish.

From my balcony so far above the yellow leaves falling from autumn, it is a mystery that man should be bred with wayward-ness in his character, that the brain may consider such fine-razored thoughts as free will. Is thought an advantage? Is it what all of nature has been leaning to for a billion years since the change of iron released the oxygen necessary for life? Beneath my station, the dark-coated sockeye stand clear from steely silvers and steelhead, from the great chinook that muscle along, large as my leg and thick as my chest. This will be a night of intermittent sleep, as it is before any of my days with rod and river — a night of forbearance, hesitation. I had been phoned by Jack Purdy of Hawkeye Marine Group and asked, "Would you come and prove the sockeye?" How could I refuse, and of course, I didn't want to.

Jack's River Lodge stands in mature Douglas-fir and cedar on the best fishing of the Somass River system north of Port Alberni on Vancouver Island. I have been invited here before the lodge has opened, to prove the summer sockeye will receive the summer fly.

My guide Nick Hnennyj's (rhymes with pennies) job is to develop the fishery — to deduce the technique, to develop and indicate the flies. As I stand on the cedar deck it's clear the lodge will develop tradition in decades to come, with jetboats and helicopters, farm-grown herbs and vegetables and 7,000-bottle wine cellar, for a corporate audience from around the world.

So it is not without trepidation that I lay myself down among the carefully selected Canadiana, the period furniture and first-edition Hemingways. All night long chinook fall through my dreams. "What is that?" I say and jerk awake when they hit the river.

Head down in the dark I pass the humming hot tub, the stainless gutting tables and down the long white stairs. Nick rows me to a rock held firmly by snags, the metatarsals of a drowned man. An eerie metaphor as the sun rises and I am surrounded by water, green and dark and deeper than a man.

Nick ties a Popsicle on my tippet and I begin to cast: first to rising fish, then across the sliding water so the fly sweeps in an arc as it drops. As though unaware of its presence, the sockeye swim by and I groan. There are fish all around me. Thousands of them.

"I don't think this is a good plan," Nick says as I wipe frustration from my forehead. He points out that sockeye, as noted in the previous essay, cease feeding when they enter freshwater. Hence their bite should not be related to the need to eat. It is also true that sockeye eat plankton composed of minute sea organisms; the largest of these are euphasid shrimp, which are clear except for pink and orange in their legs and antennae and egg masses. In other words, pink should be the colour. By now we have tried the Tequila Sunrise, Showgirl, Babine Special, Crystal Worm, Purple Marabou, Squamish Poacher, Firefly, Davie St. Hooker and, Nick's special, "The Green Thing."

Sitting on the wash of water-rounded stones, we eat our wilted cheese and lettuce sandwiches, shrug off sweaty waders. "To our right is a three- to six-foot-deep run and that is a good steelhead lie, but there are few sockeye." I can barely make out the wavering streaks to which Nick refers. "To our left," he continues, "it looks black where the two rivers join. That's actually sockeye." I am amazed. I had assumed the colour reflected a deepening of water and deposited detritus. "That's where we'll catch fish." Nick tells me he has not targeted sockeye before, other than flossing at Paper Mill Dam, closer to town, but that as a rule, migratory fish have to be taken off guard. "That spot pushes the fish together as they wait to pass up the Sproat at night. The current sweeps past them in that oxygen-rich water. Sometimes they snap at something that goes by so quick they don't get a proper look."

Soon we are standing up to our thighs in water so clear it curves our legs like something from a dream. Soon my season of unpractice annoys me. Patiently, Nick offers pointers: that I am not letting the line load up behind me; that instead of pushing my hand as though it contained a lever, I am snapping down. This, I tell him, is frustration. In an effort to cast farther I am breaking my wrist, rather than a snap to stop, resulting in the whoosh of a missile past my ear. My arm and the 5-weight just won't do the trick.

Nick points out a six-foot slick halfway across the river. "The fly has to land in there so it can sink enough to be among the fish at eye level. Maybe mend upstream, but let the current do its work."

We cast side by side, he first and then I over top. The first sockeye sizzles his line downstream. Then another. Fly placement needs to be so precise that landing three feet short of the slick translates into zero fish. The zone is the three- to eight-foot bottom, a strip 15 feet long.

Standing deep and braced against the current, I am having difficulty getting height with my line. Tomorrow the 8-weight.

Later, I rise up the stairs and set down my rod. I tell myself it's senseless to feel beaten, it's a trick of the ego, a balloon that bursts. The sky darkens and a special bottle is brought from the cellar, my favourite chardonnay, Sebastiani, 1994. It is late as the Big Dipper swings across the sky, and later still as northern lights swirl across my mind. I climb the central staircase assuring myself tomorrow will be another day.

Fish splash into my sleep and it is 5:00 AM again. I drink tea on the deck while bats whirl from the dark, their feathery flight like thoughts that barely occur. I have to admit we made progress: we nailed the technique; we nailed the flies. After going through a long list of them, Nick happened upon a delightfully simple preparation, made easily at the vise with a minimum of materials.

As I stand beside the Somass, stray thoughts cohere. They tell me my chances will improve should the slick be plumbed from the opposite bank. In the soft morning I wade out upon the shelf of rock. And then I stop, for at pool's head a black bear lifts its head, water slipping from its beard. After much eyeing one another I return to the nearest tree. When I look up, I am alone with the dawn and with the river that keeps repeating its journey. Fifty feet out I stand on the edge in calf-deep water, left foot anchored in a pie-shaped depression.

The small slick is almost directly upstream but the joining rivers will sweep my offering away from me. I crunch two BB split shots on my tippet. This makes casting more difficult but provides enough sinking power to carry the fly to fishing depth. My left hand bears a blister on its heel, proof I have been casting with my hand curled toward me rather than as an extension of my arm. Pressing against my palm, the rod had slipped, resulting in reduced transmission of power to line.

In the shallows, sockeye swim round my feet. The slitheriness of their flesh brushes my bare leg but I resist dipping the fly; these fish will not bite. I cast for the slick and the fly bumps through the pool, following the flyline in a curve. The touch had been a bite, the passive mouth of a sockeye. I cast again and strike the first flutter. Fly line zings like wire downstream. The sockeye runs into the backing before I can give chase.

The next cast the same. The sockeye strikes two seconds after the fly hits the water, runs right to my feet. With my hands high above my head, the rod snaps to the left as the fish runs the Sproat shallows. When finally subdued, it lies in the lee of a rock, a six-pound sockeye.

The sun in its majesty lifts upon the sky and my accuracy improves. Soon the flies we nickname the Pink Nick, Green Jack and Orange Dennis are landing with regularity in the slick above me. My rod tip follows the sinking line. The next fish hits so hard the flyline slices my finger and blood plunks the water. I lead the fish through the shallows, another six-pound sockeye in smolting mode — green snouted, hook jawed, purple tinged.

I sit on a rock 50 feet offshore in knee-deep water — strange to know that in winter it will be 10 feet below the surface. While my feet dangle, sockeye laze below, stacking up before the Sproat. Fully above, the sun does its fiery work upon the fish. It tires them, and it tires me. But at this edge of my education, I can do nothing with myself but stand and cast, and retrieve and cast, watching my line sweep in the pushing currents. And it happens that my reflexes learn another level of swiftness. So much so I catch a freshwater mussel, the hook having touched the only aperture between the shells — how to calculate the odds of such an occurrence?

Later, shadows reach my feet. I cast six times and receive six fish. The first runs right to the opposite shore, then upstream, snaking from riffle into pool. The last connects with current, pulling hard against the tippet. So quick it is to purpose, I cannot recover the reel. I strip with my hand and hold with my lips. I shall not forget the silence of this afternoon, fish after fish on my lips. Not the tick of reel, not the spilling water.

Then the light begins to fail and with it my ability to spot the landing fly. I move to deeper water on the shifting rocks where rivers meet. A cool hand of water brings the memory of a bear. After this day of sockeye, I am covered with slime and back exposed as I draw another from the gradient of its lie.

When I can see no longer, as happens when you're compromised, the last fish hits and steals the flyline before I can move. Across the slippery ledges in knee-deep water I run with the rod held high. I slither 200 yards until my left foot twists. Here I lie face down, hands held out, refusing to lose. I get my legs again and 200 yards farther turn the sockeye before it can slip the rapid into disappearance. Only after I release the hook on this fine, nine-pound sockeye do I realize my leg is covered in blood.

A day of indelible memory: 34 sockeye hooked and battled, 22 of these landed and released by hand. Blood dripping into the water, I am simply the first of many stories, the first in a long tradition for this fine new lodge. After a day in the swirling river, my eyes are in motion. I step from the Somass proven and the land swims by me.

Where Fish and Cars Collide

I dreaded that first robin so
but he is mastered now
　　　—Emily Dickinson, Poem Number 348

I grew up in Alberta in the 1960s, my life ruled by land and sky, an equation of blue and yellow in the often-dry prairies south of Calgary. A simple horizon of possibility, but not so simple the life that was lived in a time when hair was for the flaunting and for political statement. It was the only time when doing drugs could honestly be construed as experimenting with consciousness and the development of man and his place in the universe. Such a golden, naïve time it seems, looking back. And looking now, how we have strayed from our conversion: Lexus automobiles for adults, cell phones for every child.

I had the good fortune of living on the cliff over Fish Creek where falcons made the sky a cubist dimension. Their flight was not the softened circle of eagle or of larger hawks with their fingertips feeling the pulse of air. The cliff was always mine, and there I sat through summer, chin on my knees, brown hair pushed this way and that by heat come up the sandstone where fledglings held onto their vertical world, waiting for sinew of gopher, of hare. My own world wound away from me, to the east and disappearing into the Bow River. Upstream, the creek curved through cottonwood, rolling, benchland cattle country. To the west, a five-mile trek to the Indian reserve. These two boundaries, water and politics, were the borders of my immediate universe.

And within that universe I descended to the stream that filled the summer trough of valley with mist on evenings of stars that were a ragged tattoo in the sky. I spent my days and nights and finally years understanding each and every rock along the 10-mile course of my world: how the fish would hang behind and hang in front of obstructions, in heads of pools, in the bellies and in the foam-covered back waters I now call, having become a coastal angler, tailouts.

My memories of this time are indelible, they will not leave, etched as they are in my head so clearly they are part of my identity: running the skree beneath the cliff at full and out-of-control speed, my foot aiming to land directly on the head of the biggest snake I have ever seen. In a kind of magic of the natural, my foot pushed off the air so that I kept on flying right over it. Only my hand touching a log kept me from face-firsting it on the 45-degree slope. I came to rest at the bottom of a clay bank the stream had busily tongued away. In its face, layers of buffalo bones from centuries before, evidence that aboriginals used my cliff as a buffalo pound, driving them from the grassland above that still, more than century later, was covered in huge depressions from buffalo dust-bathing in gopher-hole tailings. And then there was the trout suspended in the magnifying lens of water before a perfect cube of sandstone fallen from the cliff one day to within inches of me; jumping around on my hands and knees after grasshoppers in the nodding spear grass; impaling a grasshopper on a size 12 Snelled hook and walking directly down the middle of the stream to make the fish spook downstream, hopper 15 feet in front of me; a fish, rainbow or cutthroat, shooting silver into my eyes; my line across the dawn ...

Above the valley bottom we lived with coyotes and deer and bad-tempered badgers walking across our lawn. When the shrill laugh of coyotes rose in unison from western ridges, I would open the sliding door to my room and imitate. As soon as the prairie sky transmitted my coyote howl, the voices of night would stop to listen and be disturbed into silence. Then my eyes closed and I went to sleep. Sometimes flaying knives strayed into my young boy's dreams, a hundred years from where they separated meat from its skin.

Into this blue-sky history I came, down the geometric CP Rail fence line a mile from the nearest road, on a track made only by our tire wheels. In winter, snow blew in rivers that compacted so hard we could jump on them and not break through. Then there is their white-squeaking sound, under moonlight, at 30 below, Northern Lights zinging around the sky. In spring the ruts were so deep I could take my hands off the wheel of my 1961 red (and in some places blue) Volkswagen Beetle. The ruts would carry the car along at speed for the entire mile and not need my steering.

It was those days and seasons that forged my connecting automobiles with fish. Those were the days when I came to understand there was nothing so bad on any road that could not be cured with a little speed. And so, the Texas gate that marked the beginning of our property became a springboard for a car that left the Earth, though only for a short time, at 60 miles an hour, before nosing into the ruts that would take me true and sure all the way home.

This red Beetle had a blue fender. It had a gas heater that could, in time, warm the heart of a musk ox. It had a hammer for days when the tires went flat with cold and the snow protested under siren lights. I whacked out two inches of ice beneath my driver's pedal so it would not stick on full, requiring me to put my head under the inch-thick dash as I drove and whack and whack until ice flew up in chunks.

My metal companion spouted burned socks from the heater holes and it did, at maximum speed, on a completely calm day, 68 miles per hour flat out, foot to the floor, on highways that snaked from Calgary to the trout that would come to focus my attention; this was the decade when we believed we teenagers were changing the world, but, instead, changed ourselves far more. Oh, to be young again. To believe we could change everything, a belief every young person should feel when they most grow.

In this time, though I apprehended the conjunction of fish and car, I did not perceive the danger. One time, falling back to Earth, the Texas gate like a kind of NASA gantry, I hit the springtime bog so hard that mud covered the windshield from side to side. At 60 miles an hour, I casually switched the wiper as I roared on, trusting in the way that only a teenager can, beneath the level of consciousness, in his ability to remain unharmed. Just as casually — on another day I would not have bothered — I glanced out the side window only to find that in the few hours I had been away, someone had come along with a backhoe and dug an eight-foot-deep hole halfway into the road bed.

At 60, windshield covered, I swerved to the right and my rear end slid left. Then the steering wheel turned back into the skid and a tremendous thump shuddered through the car. I came to rest skidding down the mud sideways across the ruts. Picking my way back through the goo, I could see my rear tire had come so close that it left a dent in the end of the hole. Had I not swerved, the car would have dived into the hole at eight miles slower than its full speed and plastered my facial skin and teeth and nose and the rest of my skull on the windshield in the split-second before it burst through and my neck cut its way down the windshield until my head was severed and rolled into the ruts of mud. Neat, I thought. And so, it was no surprise that, in pursuit of the wily rainbow and speckled trout, the splake and lake and whitefish and pike and perch, my Beetle was a little out of the realm of reality when I descended the Morley Flats hill, foot buried in the floor boards. I watched the needle revolve past 90 mph — the highest speed on the speedometer — and continue around the bottom of its circle so it came to butt against the needle marking 0 mph. In other words, the needle prevented me from seeing just how fast I could get that bug moving on the steep double hill.

And of course, on the old highway through Cochrane and Ghost River and on to Exshaw, I had a brainwave: though I could only go 68 on the flat, and would slow down to 40 up the hills where cars I just passed collected angrily in my rear-view mirror, if I drove at full speed down the hills I could still maintain a pretty good spin on the way up. Viewed this way, cars were simply obstacles that had to be gotten around and sped away from before their occupants could glower my way.

So I simply drove at max speed, building momentum down hills, and passed every car as though it was standing still. I drove through my teens and early 20s, passing on double yellow lines, passing on corners, passing through intersections and passing on the right in the shoulder, right wheel spraying gravel and slithering from the paved bed. In pursuit of fish, I left humanity standing in my slipstream.

Seemed a pretty sound plan and through the years, my many mortal scrapes with stupidity didn't register. I moved through my adult life coming closer to a bull's eye. The time, for instance, that I first fished the San Juan River west of Victoria, traversing 55 miles of twisty, windy blacktop backbone of the western edge of Vancouver Island.

So many times I have slowly opened my mind in the glow of my green lights, tea cup bearing caffeine on the dash, its steam upon the window. The rain would wash the sleep away and leave me sharpening incisors. And rain was the bearer of good news. Coho are best caught when it's pouring and that San Juan time, the skies had opened and dropped two inches in the day and continued into the night when I received the call to be at the Harris Creek bridge at 7:00 AM. So I streaked at paint-shredding speed through fog thick enough to slow the car's progress and into plastering Noah's Ark rain that promised the land would never be dry. It washed the green out of evergreen.

Long before dawn and the first travellers were on the road, I zipped the high passage somewhere west of Loss Creek, windshield wipers blurring my indistinct view of the black reality outside. A line from Emily Dickinson had been playing and replaying in my mind: "I dreaded that first robin so." In her world, that line is about aging and how, when we reach the markers of that, we come to know we have less time to go than when the last marker was crossed.

Though I recalled that line of poetry, I could not recall the next. And then, at 50 mph, I discovered the curve was a fall-away one and a river ran across the pavement. I touched the brakes and the car hydroplaned directly across the oncoming lanes.

Passing through the ditch in an instant I would later reconstruct to understand, my car hit rocks the size of baby carriages. This threw it into the air so that, my fingerprints embedded in the wheel, we flew sideways. As I looked down through the passenger window, the bottom of the car hit the mountain so hard it ricocheted me back through the ditch of rocks onto the highway, brakes locked. I came to a skidded stop: one tire exploded, two rims destroyed, six lug nuts sheared off, blinker-light assembly pushed in six inches, a line of blood running down my chin and, in the blackest part of black, as though nothing at all had happened. A hubcap twiddled like a wa-wa dying nickel by the car. And, as I found out, a diagonal crater ran two inches deep from behind one wheel across the bottom of the car to the opposite door.

But at the moment my mind was focussed elsewhere and I hurled the retrieved cap into the back seat of my beat-up Subaru and increased my pace so I wouldn't be late for my date with fish. Pulling hard right on the steering wheel, I zapped the last 15 miles through the sleeping town of Port Renfrew, across the wide estuary, the rolling gravel and patched asphalt and screeched to a 7:30 AM halt along the ditch.

The dead tire and tooth-knocked-out rim were changed and I was left in the rain with the river some 10 feet above its banks and brown, carrying stumps with their rigging of roots like dying empresses grinding down freestones the size of basketballs. And then a day of complete wilderness, keeping my camera alive in pontoon side baskets filled with rain and catching 20-pound coho. After, the slog from the ballooned river, pontoon boats on our soaked shoulders, through the mud-bottom swamp toward the truck.

Back at the car, I discovered that one wheel went shoo-thump shoo-thump, and slowly I shoo-thumped my way back to Victoria, noting, when I drove by the rock face that had bent the bottom of my car, that in its flight the car had cut off a couple dozen 20-foot alders in its trajectory and neatly clipped a sign and its four-by-four into splinters.

After the 55 miles I discovered that the shoo-thump tire had only one lug nut left and it had worn a hole in the rim so large it was close to passing through itself and swerving me into oncoming traffic had it in its judgment chosen to do so. At this point I finally decided that even though I was perfectly safe in the perfect, undisturbed and complete harmoniousness of my immediate stuffed-with-karma universe, I could not count on the world, the other drivers, the air, the trees, the animals and all the rocks and cliffs, etc.

My mechanic, lying under the car surveying the gouges, the switch-light assembly pushed back, said only one thing, through whistled breath, "You were lucky you weren't killed." I decided to reform and, because the rest of humanity and the universe were not up to keeping up with me, I would slow down and ensure my own safety.

But of course, there are always more stories and one has to be judicious in picking out the ones that lead to the point where fish and cars collide. In my 50th year, I went out to the Stamp River in my brand new, dry-in-five-minutes duds, recently bought and wishing to be tried out. As well, this was the first time I would use my new Diamondback 8-weight in pursuit of the mystical and beautiful steelhead.

Above the Robertson Creek Hatchery island, I eased into the wide run with gravel that slid out beneath my feet as I braced against the waist-high flow. As luck would have it, my first cast was mended upstream and under connection when the confident stop of my first steelhead erupted into my brain's pleasure centre. I grudgingly gave ground, heels in the splaying gravel, body going through holes so deep my packsack went under and the water came to my neck until my stripping hand could grasp a soft sweeper before a pool much deeper than I opened. I skidded the shoreline of the island, past chum carcasses, the vertebrae and the jawbones, the keta teeth sitting on stumps, and all the way down to the hatchery fence.

This plastic fence is used in the fall when it is lifted and forms a barrier that makes chinook and coho turn and swim into the hatchery channels a third of a mile below, on the lower end of the lagoon. On this May morning, it shimmered on the bottom, diamond crisscrosses of bright orange mesh. I landed the steelhead in the middle of the river, standing on the fence where in its lee gravel built up to only waist deep before opening up into the lake.

As I swung my hips across the current so as to retrace my steps, one toe stubbed one diamond and my other leg, as though in wind beyond its strength, lifted and was held, flying in the water. On one toe, I was a human prayer wheel. My hand came down to hold and, of course, went through the water surface and I turned so that my back faced the current, one foot still in the wind. I was a headless chicken for half a minute on the edge of eternity until my second foot came and settled securely, allowing me to edge across the river on the laid-down fence.

And then the upstream trek through water to my ribs. In the lee of the island, thousands of fry in their element, nibbling my calves under my pants. I found I could not stop shaking, not out of fear, but simply because I was cold. I had not considered, when forsaking my sweaty neoprenes, that I was also forsaking warmth so I was now becoming illogical. My chest and my legs pulled into the middle of my body as though on strings and I could not walk upstream in the water. I forced myself over logs in a skunk cabbage swamp and through walls of vegetation that chose to keep hold of the tip of my rod. When I came to the final crossing I was so uncoordinated with cold I knew I might not make it.

But I did, slowly, legs unconnected to my head, hand over hand, holding a log in the press of water, on my pack and back, up to the muddy path where I lay frozen on a sunny, late-spring day. Lying in the forest, at this time, I discovered — you will recall this is a story about cars — that my keys were not in my pocket. My previous good practice was to put my keys on their float (so they wouldn't drop off the dock on days I went out in my boat on the ocean) in my wader's pocket, which was sealed with a zipper, so I knew at all times where they were.

I had lost feeling below my knees and in trying to run down the trail I was a stumbling, drunken collision with gravity until I found a patch of sunlight. There I went through every pocket in my clothes — these expensive, dry-in-no-time clothes have 11 pockets — but no key. I then went through every pocket in my packsack and emptied the contents of the bag. No key. Then I went through every pocket in my clothes and packsack two more times. Still no key.

Knowing it was getting close to 4:00 PM when the gates are closed and I would be stuck in the dark, frozen, 25 miles from Port Alberni with only bears for company, I trudged on to my car where a further search turned up nothing. There was no point in breaking a window as I did not have a key in my car.

And then it dawned on me what had happened. This was the first time I had worn my nifty new duds and I had put my keys, with their float, in a front pocket without a zipper, clasp, button or etc. While I had been giving myself hypothermia, they simply and naturally floated up out of my pants and down the river, never to be seen again.

At the hatchery, the lights were going out. It was suggested to me that I phone a locksmith, but nary a locksmith could be found. I phoned BCAA, but they told me I wasn't a member. I phoned my ICBC Roadstar people, but was told that unless my car was stolen, they could not help me. And the Greyhound bus would not come where I was and would not get me home until early the next morning.

Water draining out of my boots onto the linoleum, I phoned the only Port Alberni person I knew, and not very well, and asked him to lend me a car. He hummed and hawed in surprise trying to think of a way to get out of this unnatural imposition out of the blue from a distant friend of a friend.

"How about renting a car?" he said and then it dawned on me, this one obvious lifesaving solution that I, in my frozen state, could not have thought of — that's how out of it my brain was. So it came to pass that Darren Delucca came to my rescue and deposited me at Budget Rent a Car, where I did, indeed, rent a car.

That is why I now have five car keys: one in a magnetic container attached (and also taped) to the radiator; one tied on a line from the inside of the hood; one tied on a line under the driver's seat; one on my chain of spiffy fishing tools; and one with my other keys.

This taught me to consider for the first time that, with all the fish-catching stuff I had learned over the decades, I ought not take the chances that I regularly did. It was time to put this experience into the keep-alive pigeonhole; I had learned not to walk across logs 15 feet off the ground, for if I fell and broke my leg, I would be found there as whitened bones if ever a part of me were found again. Or gorier, impaled on a broken branch that I fell off the log and onto. Or the six-foot-diameter log in the San Juan bush I had slithered under and thought, precisely at the bottom of the trip, that if it shifted even a few inches I would be pinned and dead before the search party realized I had not left any sort of plan at home or a phone message to say which corner of the 50,000 square miles of Vancouver Island bush they could start looking in.

Or I sort of learned this. Having passed up and down the highway too many dozen times in the dark, I finally found that no matter how maniacally I drove, there was no point in doing so; once started up the Malahat Drive 20 miles from Victoria, I could drive down the passing lanes at 90 mph and still, by the winding downhill section, all the cars I had almost killed myself to pass would slowly form up behind me in a line and then, embarrassingly, be beside me at the first red light in Langford on the way into town.

So the collision of fish and car had the quality of a new day, that is, a new sun clicking on in my brain like a kind of intelligence. My final lesson of them all (or so I claim now) came on the Cameron Lake section of the road that passes over the summit from Port Alberni to Parksville.

In keeping with my 30-year tradition of being the fastest car on the road in the lowest powered of them all, I found myself on the curvy, mountain-loaded portion of the road, fast catching logging trucks. Knowing there was a passing lane just off the end of the lake where the Little Qualicum dropped with its load of brown trout, I pulled out with my foot on the floor, making the cats' eyes blips under my wheels. I cruised past the first logging truck at 80 mph and at that moment, caught the right lane merge sign as I flashed past it and found, much to my chagrin, my knuckles now white on the steering wheel, there was a van ahead of the logging truck which I had no time to slow down for and I charged right on by. When I tried the brakes, smoke appeared in my mirror as the car slid like a pear on ice. I would hit the second semi load of lumber at easily a difference of 30 mph.

At that point I simply hit the gas and of course the car, and all of its too few horsepower, didn't respond. The extra right lane in front of the semi was ending and I had no choice but to continue, straining for 90 mph. The semi started to merge as I was beside its load, pushing me slowly across the centre line into the oncoming lanes. The semi had no choice as we were approaching a bridge that had only two lanes.

Drawing even with the cab, I realized that a third semi was barrelling down on me from the other direction. Firmly between the two semis, travelling at the speed of sound, I was, for that instant, the skeletons in *Trains and Planes and Automobiles* that John Candy and Steve Martin become. The three of us abreast in the middle of the bridge, I pulling in with a foot to spare before I became strawberry jam, I rolled on, sweating the thin sweat of spiders in the fall.

But then, only a few miles farther on, by which time I hoped to escape the wrath of the loggers behind me, I came upon a long line of cars, and no matter how many brave and ill-considered maneuvres I made, I could not pass a single one all the way to the clover-leaf entrance to the highway near Qualicum.

The semi I risked death to pass was right on my ass end, so close I could read the bugs on his licence plate. I knew, at that moment, there had been no point in risking my life and that it was time, once and for all, entering my fifth decade and the second half of my finite life, to slow down before the probabilities of being pasted like a mosquito grew long. With my many years of wisdom I had to admit that driving like there was no tomorrow would simply ensure that that was true.

And to my amazement, when I queried the League of Canadian Poets list-serve about the next line of Dickinson's poem, a bizarre bit of synchronicity. Her next line is: "but he is mastered now." After 35 years of slightly not-sane driving, I've finally grown up enough to slow down from the sonic-boom speeds I have travelled in the dark en route to a fish.

I am old enough to know that I and my generation couldn't change the world. All a person can ask for is to change himself, and that is the eternal bit of truth there is to be sought and gained after the Second World War blew itself up each Sunday on Walter Cronkite's show *20th Century.*

Speed is mastered now. I have slowed down — on paved roads. On the potholey, dusty, muddy, washboardy, gravel Nitinat road, I spend my darkened mornings and evenings racing to and from the fish, averaging a measly 50 mph. Yes, still I pass — in fact, I have never been passed — but far more slowly than I have ever done before. I pass, because I know that the first person to the river is the lucky bird. But those stories of cars are stories of another book — my infatuation with the Nitinat River — and my maroon Subaru that forced apart trees and drove down streams to get there.

To Understand or Not to Understand is Not the Question

It's simply a part of the brain, I tell myself, not the past I remember so well. Pulling up recalcitrant neoprene I resist what I have read in journals, even though I have to accept its truth. Scientists using positron emission tomography now tell us that we do not remember memories from the past; rather they are constructed on the spot at the time we think them. Hmm: Instant memory; spontaneous memory; today's memory versus today's memory of yesterday's memory? Yes, perhaps that's it.

I remember clearly the first fish I ever saw, a small brook trout lifted from knee-deep water within bending poplar trees along a small Alberta stream whose name I can no longer recall. Today's memory — as contradictory as that may sound and assuming I believe the assembly-into-engrams as Orwell labelled thoughts — offers a heavy density of shade. The scene registered in my five-year-old eyes and ears as an extension of the living room in our post-war bungalow. I remember it as though a trout stream flowed for my enjoyment between the old green couch and the wooden RCA with its black-and-white test pattern, its Indian chief in feather headdress.

And I cannot forget the summers of Richard Brautigan, his novel *Trout Fishing In America*, nor his wonderful and sad suggestion that trout streams could be found in dusty warehouses, taken apart in sections and leaned against the wall, waiting, waiting but never being found. Never being purchased. His *In Watermelon Sugar* is possibly the sweetest, vaguest, most charismatic little tome from the mental state that was the '60s; along with *Jonathan Livingston Seagull* (now hokey and sentimental as spun-sugar frosting), it convinced us that we could achieve anything. How we believed that one line in that little book, rejected by publishers more than 50 times, was meant for us alone, our generation lost in space: "We tackle flying through rock a little later in the program."

We, with our acidized eyes, never saw that we were simply aspiring to the shibboleth of, the hubris of American ideals; they were formed long before and passed across scores of generations from Greece five centuries before the Son of the God of the Christian, of the Judeo-Christian religion, was born a man. A long long time. A long long development. We in our green skins thought we were originals.

In that time, that room of the mind, we truly believed we were agents for universal change, when we dropped and smoked and injected drugs for mankind. And then there's today. Would our kids be embarrassed for us? Would they laugh at our juvenility? Would they think that must be why we "stopped trying" and became staid and adult? And what about us? Would we be embarrassed? Are we? I don't think so. There's no point in being embarrassed, only point in learning not to do it again. Oh, yes, whether it's today's, or yesterday's or another's remembrance?

Give me strength to say I don't care what I don't understand, to declare what may well be untrue: I say the fish and the human part of human nature should reside close by. To save my ageing eyes the impossibility of adding an intermediate sink tip, 10-pound tippet and

Improved Clinch Knot (which at the best of times can outfox my eyes and fingers) by the ceiling light of my almost-new 1991 white Subaru station wagon (after my maroon one went the way of the dispossessed), I assemble my gear the previous evening.

The Blood knot between the mono sections I have long tossed away for the simpler but weaker Double Surgeon's knot. And with the experience of salmon larger than 50 pounds, I now have come to decide that linked sections with loops formed by Figure Eight knots are stronger than the other knots.

So strong is the Figure Eight that to my amazement, one day after settling a favourite fly in a nondescript bush on the other side of the river, I pointed the rod tip at it and began backing up. Up the gravel I stepped until the line popped and I was sitting on my rear end, the flyline snapped into my face. And the result? Ah, that the Nailless Nail knot between the gossamer and the flyline had separated while six-pound test and Figure Eight had not.

Apparently, the small amygdala connects the images of the visual cortex, the input of the reptilian cerebellum and adds emotion stored elsewhere in the brain to "construct," in the here and now, a memory that we receive as though it is an exact copy of an event that may have occurred some decades before. I remember Blood knots, though I can no longer see them. And now, when securing a fly, I do so with an Improved Clinch Knot and can only put the mono through the eye because I have done it, like riding a bicycle, a million times over my life.

I add that it all mushes together as I step into the darkened river where De Mamiel Creek and the Sooke River empty into one another. The soft conversation of their night voices rises in mist and I am willing to believe I have come to the waters for some deeper purpose, one that is largely hidden, and one that need not be deciphered.

Casting my gaze up and down after night's darkest hour, I do not see any chum, coho or chinook salmon. My eyes come to rest on the riffle beneath my feet, and after a few moments it becomes clear that the small sticks in the tumbling water are actually dorsal fins. Now the adrenaline that keeps me awake each night before my date with a fishing rod moves my left arm to cast the fly. And in stepping forward in calf-deep water, I almost fall into the dark over a chinook as long and thick as a log.

In the small glow arriving, I toe the wavering fish, but it does not react. On a whim, I tuck my rod under my arm and reach down. My hands close around the wrist of its tail and it serpentines into the dark. Poetry comes back to me now: "It is morning and I am kneeling/in the garden watching the green/bodies lift into light." Such pure religion in those three Patrick Lane lines.

Hands liberally coated with fish slime, I look up into a set of eyes. Black eyes in a black face. The bear looks down at me on my knees in the morning. No doubt I smell sweet to him so far from a climbable tree. All I can do is look away from predatory eyes.

As fate would have it, the bear turns and moves until it merges with the dark. And there I am on my hands and knees in front of hundreds of salmon finning the nervous water. There is nothing left to do but rise up and cast, even though it no longer matters whether a fish is hooked. I am complete. In the here and now.

A few minutes later my White Woolly Bugger connects with dog salmon jaw and an 18-pound buck leaves craters in the dawn. I do not understand such a conjunction of events and do not care to. I am prepared to accept my memories as the worn truth of the past and the sound of water that lures me to them again and again. I will accept anything.

Taking the Slow Way Home

As the eagle flies from Vancouver, airplanes land in two hours at Prince Rupert's island airport. The journey home at nine knots per hour down the Inside Passage is a satisfying alternative return to civilization.

Giving in to caprice, this journey of days can stretch for weeks. If every jot of island, fjord and inlet is lined in a row, more than 12,000 miles of shoreline stretches out the road less travelled — and more enjoyed. Whether by sailboat or other displacement-hulled craft — my transit is by fish packer — the slow Victoria wend is a worthwhile indulgence in wanderlust.

At the foot of the mountain, Prince Rupert is an evening blanket. The town was named after the dashing cousin of King Charles II by the ill-fated and grandiosely titled Grand Trunk Pacific Railway Company. Francis Mawson Rattenbury, our own architect of the "Parliament" Buildings and Empress Hotel in Victoria, joined the company and designed its wooden-structure hotel.

Though the rail line was visionary, the First World War intervened and resulted in both the company's and Rattenbury's demise. In a friendly conspiracy both had purchased land in the valley approaches, expecting windfall profits, and this expectation proved the beginning of the end of the incandescent career Rattenbury previously enjoyed.

At the dawn of my own pulling out, conveyor belts of ice crash into blue plastic totes in a surreal halogen-gleam of lights. The *Ocean Investor*, our 85-foot, 110-ton packer, slips its Port Edward lines and travels down the northern sun en route to Princess Royal Island and sightings of the Kermode Spirit Bear, a white genetic sibling to other island bears. At nine knots the traveller truly has the time to wait and discover such rarities. But I am also on a working vessel and that means days of running down channels: Grenville, Fitz Hugh and Seaforth. Down a landscape of white-headed mountains with waterfalls falling into mist before they can hit the ground.

And days of beautiful, haunted trees, heads of Sitka spruce worried into dreadlocks by relentless wind that blows the winter through. These trees, so like old Japanese men: lone fingers of white that will never be "harvested" because lumbermanese designates them "decadent" and not worth the shearing of a mountain.

We spend the first night in Hartley Bay where the Gitga'ata First Nation has erected a boardwalk structure all around the town, with entrances like slips on a dock to the built and unbuilt houses. Pilings rise from muskeg for house and school and central ceremonial hall, the latter with timbers 20 feet tall and three feet wide, every inch bearing the nubbling of adze that is a trademark of Indian carving. We deliver salt for drying black cod and halibut and are sent off with so many trays of cinnamon buns that I subsist on this "fifth food group" the rest of the voyage. On our leaving, pellets of April snow descend. We look back at a town on stilts where 22 feet of white fell last winter and had people skiing off their houses. The *Ocean Investor* pulls at its tethers and a solitary line of bootprints curves across the float.

But also out here is a sea-surrounded land where other dreams have had to be let go. Like a Streisand and Redford *The Way We Were* flashback, the empty, sore towns where human life has rung, and then succumbed to the soft, insistent, decades of rain. Nature in its slow, methodical absorption of man's efforts to struggle a bit from the Earth has reclaimed Butedale, Namu, even Ocean Falls.

Butedale has houses some nighttime giant picked up in his hand and dropped like toys. These houses line the old harbour, off their moorings, turning to the sun-robbed silver that is paint retired to anonymity. Under one deck evidence of recent man: bucked and split logs with buttery yellow hearts. A boat pulled up the rocks and a house with its face twisted on its pilings.

One evening we lash to the overhead hopper of the eerily empty Namu. The next morning a small skeleton crew gives evidence of continued efforts to revive what nature has taken back. Up on the tin roofs the men shovel moss off the gables into three-foot drifts where the green sponge hits the ground. Then the empty houses, the empty side-by-sides, the bachelors' quarters in the cheerily named Namu Hilton and Convention Centre. Then factories where more than a hundred people worked to transform the sea's prodigious delivery of salmon and seafood for a hungry world. Everywhere, clamshells stick out from the land, evidence of middens carbon-dated to more than 7,000 years old.

Today the boardwalk seeps to the ocean. Buildings leave their roots and topple face first before the simple cloth of mist once again sends them to the land from which all living things rise and must return. These are the thoughts that occur when one is separated from palm coms and email, the usual urban rush toward oblivion that is our lot.

Under the dock, after the tide has left the beach to itself, I see the emblem of remote: cast-off engine heads, rail-car wheels, unidentifiable twisted pipes, chunky gears, exhaust pipes and the oddness of one white propeller. This is mankind's leavings and the sea reclaims the shallows, covering all with a fine white sifting that is a layer of barnacles taking residence where man could not keep his foothold.

And the eye of lighthouses out here in a land and water so far away from our nation's capital that no one can hear us calling. So, warned by VHF Channel 16, we dodge a night of wind at Pruth Bay, Hakai Pass, which, simply put, is the most beautiful spot on the entire coast. But that night the gale comes down from the black so thick it digs holes in the water and pushes doors of rain across the lights' thin, short gaze. The next morning, I query whether neighbour, and captain, my captain, Gord Coutts noticed the wind in the night, and how come, if there are only two of us on board, at 3:00 AM there is a lineup for the loo? Gord just laughs at me and says he was up all night, and at one time had the axe out in aid of chopping the lines because the boat could have pulled the entire dock from its moorings.

Then the Pacific crossing, the dash past the aptly named Cape Caution, so named in May of 1793 by Captain Vancouver, his ship, *Discovery*, having nearly been lost on a rock with white-bearded waves falling back to green.

Vancouver's *Discovery* was larger than the boat we ferry along the white succession of rock: ship rigged, 340 tons, sheathed with planks and coppered. The vessel mounted 10 4-pounders and 10 swivels, with 134 crew. We are only two. Good reason in these days of electronics to travel with radar, global positioning system, VHF and depth sounder.

This is the history one sails through on the slow trip home. And although the summery months can promise calmer waters on the portion crossing the open Pacific, other months favour those who have well-developed boating skills. During our pitch-and-yaw crossing to Port Hardy, a well-placed Adida jammed against the dash and the other against the sill keep me from being a fo'c's'le projectile. We traverse a confused sea of residual 10-foot chop coming from two directions. When the wave corners meet, the beauty of them rising in a white clap another 10 feet.

Most Victorians know that Port Hardy is the southern terminus for the Inside Passage ferry that beetles at near 19 knots, a goodly clip in comparison with smaller, displacement hulls. But what I had not known, and presumably most south-island residents and those who visit from afar are the same, is that the trip from Port Hardy to Victoria is nearly the same length and beauty as the Inside Passage itself.

We see the day come twice on that 36-hour passage from Port Hardy to Victoria. As the sun fails on the first day, we trek Seymour Narrows. In 1958, the government tunnelled under Ripple Rock and blew it into fragments. Even with this improvement, the whirlpools still take vessels as large as ours today. Holes open in the rips, turn a boat on its heels and draw it down into a Joseph Conrad tale of the sea.

We pass the end of the narrows safely, well before peak flood. The sweeping arms of ocean indifference spew past Cape Mudge and fan out into Georgia Strait. In the dark, for hours, under the light of the moon, waves coming with us like glass horses set out for destinations not yet confirmed.

By the time red digs through the night, we are passing Gabriola Island and its eons of wind-and-wave-sculpted sedimentary towers. And later, slipping outside Discovery Island, named after Vancouver's vessel 50 years later in 1846 by Captain Kellett on his survey, we zigzag the odd conflicting tides of Oak Bay Flats.

Both Victoria tide and Race Rocks current play across The Flats at the same time resulting, some days, in flood and ebb waters simultaneously. In 1791, Jose Maria Narvaez, the Spanish explorer, wrote in his diary that Enterprise Channel, at Trial Island's north end, "flowed like a copious river."

And then the breakwater with white shrugging the granite blocks, Rattenbury's Parliament Buildings with strings of light down their quarried rock angles. And the knowledge that a slow traverse down B.C. history has been completed. Take time to take this time and you will come back from the other side a little less harried and a little more in touch with the wildness that is our good fortune. The sea is relinquished slowly, for when we step onto land our legs keep rolling into night.

How a Skunk Becomes a Fish

I stand alone on the dock. The engine displaces the night silence, echoes from trees on the shore. The canvas dodger is snapped free, downriggers dropped into their slots. Hooks are sharpened. The hay-smell of October fills the air.

I am going fishing with my usual partner: me. I tend not to ask people as often as I should. The reason is that I can't stand getting skunked when someone else is there. Added to this, my decision to go or not to go is no Shakespearean soliloquy — it's usually made the day before I go, i.e., too late to ask anyone else. This is rationalization, I know. But it sounds plausible, written to someone else.

I flip up the bumpers and turn to the night, to the heron, a flesh-starved statue on the rippling sand, perhaps the same one that stands frozen in the shore when I fish with Patrick Lane in winter. Above me rides the October moon, full and gold, close enough to touch. This is the moon that signifies the annual harvest: northerns coming home to renew their numbers. These are the biggest coho of the year, some exceeding 20 pounds. The run has been building through September. The clear, tea-stained autumn sky holds them in the strait and when the rains finally come, they will be gone, washed into one of 800 spawning streams in British Columbia.

The moon follows me south, past the navy wharf, past the kelp beds, past Bentinck Island. In Race Channel the sea falls so fast I can see it run downhill; such a phenomenon, a trick of the eye. Even on a calm day the sea moves with the sound of a waterfall. In the dimness, a hundred boats float by like Christmas-tree bulbs set free. I nose into Juan de Fuca Strait.

Unlike chinook, Northerns migrate some distance from land. They inhabit the top layer of water, seldom 80 feet down, in the tide lines of one, three and five miles offshore. On the American side, the last lights flutter on Ediz Hook. I prop my feet against the seat and tap the throttle to 1,000 rpm; northerns prefer their "food," their stimulator, their three-D Plaid flasher in full snap. In the early morning, light- and white-coloured lures out-produce the darker tones. The sun lifts its great red bulk from the east and melts the moon. I read coho 40 feet below, then emptiness for 300 more.

Then the quick sound of a finger and a thumb I feel before I see, the zzz of reel. My head, in the straightest line to the rod guide, connects with the door jamb and a headache. I miss the reel and it cracks my knuckles. My palm against the single-action reel, then a crescent of pain from index finger to wrist when the drum lets go. Wonderful, masterful technique here, Dennis.

The boat continues its wayward path as the fish insinuates itself under the centre line and heads resolutely to the other side of the boat. Webby feet pad the canvas above my head. Both hands occupied, I jump from the deck so my head contacts the canvas. The seagull drops off, pursuing safety.

Then the netting, two fishing lines still in the water. Two downriggers whistling their metallic tunes. Three rodholders. With my "free" hand I lower the net, and with the other, maneuvre the fish closer. Going against every article and book I have ever written — fish are always landed head first — I am reduced to chasing this fish with the net. The boat begins to curve away. And then the fish makes a fatal error: instead of getting caught in the kicker, it swims directly into the net.

With my prize slithering the deck, I race to the steering wheel through tangles of fishing line — Gulliver strung by Lilliputian ropes. In turning the fish from the net, I note that one hook is caught in the mesh and without much thought reach the long way in with my fingers and sure enough it shoots free, directly into the pad of my thumb, and of course, it is now that the coho takes slippery flight around the deck, pulling my hand with its hook. I am bonking after the fish, a bonk here, a bonk there, the hook still in my thumb and the blood vessels behind my eyeballs bulging. When I have finally bashed the bottom of my boat and the coho into submission, then I may be in submission, retrieving my flesh from the metal with my pliers.

Finger wrapped in a ripped strip of towel, I head back to the tide line, reestablish my gear. Thank God. Soon there is freedom for an early winter spring: the hook is turned upside down and the fish snapped free without having been lifted from the sea.

Now the dry-gulch phenomenon every fisher knows. Fish nothingness stretches out and the fish I let go starts to look pretty good. I follow my own advice: having started with a plan of three lures, I move to my backup plan of my next three. The anchovy is removed; strip is put in its place. Half an hour later even that is brought in.

The sun is now high overhead and the white hootchie needs replacing with a darker one — an Army Truck pattern descends. Soon it, too, needs replacement. As does a Krippled K. This is the season of the infrared spectrum. In the fall, when the sun spends much of its time lifting and falling through the warm atmosphere, red light predominates. This is also the time of fish eggs, red and defendable on spawning redds. Hence, I put out a pink Apex. An hour goes by. Still nothing.

I spend the time thinking. I need to solve two problems: what to use and where to fish. Since these are fall northerns, fishing depth is pretty well defined. Even though the strait can be 1,000 feet deep, the battlers of autumn inhabit only the upper levels and this makes the aspect of gear depth easy to solve.

It crosses my mind, as I move from one tide line to the next and then the next, fishing successively to five miles offshore, that the only coho I have on board, and slit open, is stuffed with some indefinable feed with wriggly jelly "legs" and bright black beady eyes. Ah, yes, one of the new glow lures with ultraviolet may do the trick. I take a new Mint Tulip hootchie — it has long, clear fronds — from its package and re-rig. But it too simply waves in the breeze.

Rummaging around in one of my tackle boxes — the one I reserve for hootchies — I find a rust-stained old hootchie: clear with one black stripe. I have never caught a thing on this and it looks like something I would buy only in a weak moment. My third tackle box is littered with must-have purchases that subsequently reveal themselves as useless. As it is deep fall, I put in a red spacer bead, then add another for length, i.e., to get the hook at the tippy end of the fronds.

A skunk is a condition of mind I cannot stand. And one fish is only slightly better, particularly when there is another that could have been in the boat. Hence, I am glad that I am on my own, when the tried and true does not produce the way it ought to. To add to this long day of few coho, a seagull, looking like it knows every verse of *The Rime of the Ancient Mariner,* lands for a pit stop on the bow of my boat. Dabbing Palmolive soap on an Improved Clinch Knot, I pound on the window with my elbow, shouting, "Out, damned seagull." Relieved and satisfied, it departs, leaving its stain ripening in the sun.

I turn to the second problem: finding the fish. Over the years, it has become clear to me that once you have the basics under your belt, finding the fish is probably the most important aspect of catching them. If you consider that 99 percent of the water is devoid of fish, only 1 percent of the time will you be in a position to hook one. Thus your chances improve dramatically if you can find the monsters of the green.

The past few hours have been comprised of boundless strategy and zero fish. Perhaps something will change. The tide has been rising much of the time. Many times, in fishing the 25-mile-wide channel between Washington and B.C., I have seen tide move coho as much as 15 miles. Staying in contact proves the most important part of catching them. In late October, the fish can be pushed and then deposited in a tide line that forms on a southwest diagonal off the back of Race Rocks miles into the shipping lanes and on to the American side. The fish get transported into this line and sit just on the front edge where flood tide meets falling current coming from the other direction. Over the hours more and more fish are swept into and stay in this tide line.

There is a green can buoy behind the race, marking rocks that move the water crazily. And on it sit two sea lions, a tiny little pad for two great beasts. They seem to be saying, "Here, you go first." "No, you, be my guest." And then a black obelisk lifts from the ocean. It rises eight feet and then descends those same feet down. Near by, another curved black fin, the sound of breath. And thus the reason for the sea lions being out of the water on a postage stamp of safe ground. Transient killer whales find sea lions a nice meal, basketball-sized chunks of flesh bitten out, a half-ton animal thrown like a mouse.

And they too, for all their superb strength and the beauty of their black smooth skin, the intelligence of their small eye when they lie on side examining you, are not good omens for fishing success. When they pass through, fishing declines for hours. Presumably their echolocation, their "pings," must be heard through lateral-line "ears" of salmon. Whatever the reason, salmon within a half mile in front and every salmon they have passed become too skittish to bite. There is no option but to motor "upstream" many miles and sink lines again.

It is now noon. Fishing time is short. I have only one fish to take back to criticism on the dock. The sea surges toward Victoria and the distant San Juan Islands. The boat rocks in the standing waves of the tide line. My tackle box is launched, lid open, for the floor where a hundred leaders do their best to join their brothers. Could something be better? Could the rod tip's slow descent promise anything more than a trip through the giant purple jellyfish that are liquid fire on one's skin? But no, it is not that; on the other end a white mouth closes on Mint Tulip, and closes with confidence, for the rod tip comes to lie horizontal with the water. Soon, though, the tip describes a half circle and the fish is in front of the boat, fishing line wound in the aerial, the bow line and the railing. I sense another rule coming on: a fish will foul on the smallest bird dropping, the smallest screw, the smallest footprint on the bow.

When finally subdued, the fish flops on its silver side, nosing into the net. At this point, the clear hootchy screams off and I'm standing with a fish in the net wondering what to do. The answer is to drop it and get the next fish to the boat, to boat them both in the same net at the same time, then untangle all the gear. Leaning back against the cabin wall, I sweat and recall Roderick Haig-Brown's bit of prose in which he nets a three-pound steelhead and can't believe the tension and sweat he has been in for such a small fish. Well, that is where a fisherman is. With each fish.

I lift the downrigger lines and rattle across the chop to the streaming side of the tide line. The lines are reset and I swig back some Coke as the boat crosses into rougher water. Simultaneously, both rods snap to the rear, a sure sign of a tangle. But this turns out not to be the case, as when one rod is in hand, the other is yanking asymmetrically, clear evidence of a fish on each line.

When the fish lie beside me and their bellies show white, they are identical, both 13 pounds, of the same length and girth. Northerns. They gasp in the net as I make a decision. To set free or not to set free. I'm over my limit retaining both; one will die; one will swim away. When the hook is snapped, the fish disappears, drenching my glasses with water — salt water, the old coho face wash.

Reputation intact — I guess it's only with me, the internal critic — from a zero-looking morning, I have come up with a catch for more than one person, and released the extras for the second. A common horn of plenty for one in this late autumn day, scented with smoke of fire lifting from the shore. A harvest of fall. A boat full of fish, I resolve to risk a skunk the next time out. A promise that, for the moment, I know I will keep. The boat planes for home, safe moorage, the great blue heron poised to strike.

Is There a Benign Mythology of Colour That Accounts for All This Ice?

Patrick and I crunch the salt-strewn gangplank. January stretches out white and silent, a kind of statue of a world forgotten. In the night the seasonal stream has floated out over the sea and frozen, turning the harbour into a field of ice. It suggests a man could just walk right out and go on into the openness wherever he wanted. But that is just a trick of cold. And another: near us, a heron flaps its wings but gets nowhere, its feet frozen to the shore. It is a wild pathetic beauty.

Reluctantly, the boat cycles from cold sleep. Numb from canvas snaps, my fingers rig the newest purchases: a Coyote spoon and a Dragon Boat hootchie. I buy everything, all the new griddle-hot lures, and it is a rule I buy two — you need a second to throw on if the first gets hot. This rule my three tackle boxes prefer. They bulge with good fortune and bad — past purchases I never seem to find a reason to throw away. In the short distance from the marina I have to admit I have lost faith in the Dragon Boat. It looks more a summer red-sun lure for pink salmon than a deep, green-glow-eye chinook snagger. This is a time when January makes skeletons of everything, and it is blue in cold.

We've come in search of winter quarry. At least eight months of the year, most British Columbia saltwater locations host only one species of salmon: resident feeder chinook two to three years old, averaging 8 to 15 pounds. Each winter gives up bigger brutes that push 30 pounds of water aside. The strategy in winter is as it is in every other season: it starts with the fish and how they choose their curve of the sea. Unlike those drawn without their say, the spawners moved by summer — and that includes chinook — winter chinook stay deep and they stay put. Success, once you know the fish, comes down to thinking in the ocean's five dimensions: length, width, depth, tide and time.

I put the boat into reverse and the transom crunches the ice. From the darkened shore, a crushing sound comes back. Herons release their old-man squawks. I push the boat into forward and it moves beneath us like a horse shifting on its haunches. As we grind out of the harbour, I remove my hands from the wheel and the idling boat rides up then crunches down, ripping the harbour open like the bones of fleshless animals.

Patrick flips in the bumpers, drops the downriggers into their slots. His eyes move with the lights on shore. He draws a single Siwash hook down the stone. The boat heads itself to a series of ledges 80 to 200 feet deep. A mountain cliff under the water — sharp, downrigger-line-shredding rock drops from the penitentiary on William Head. Instinct and cruising books of past catches tell me the fish will be elsewhere but I'm of two minds. The gurus at the marina told me to try here and Patrick is Patrick Lane, the best poet in Canada. I want my fabled, my taught-Hemingway-everything-he-knew status in the fish-catching literary world intact. A skunk had better not come our way.

I'm dubious about the water beneath our keel. Over the years I have learned to look at the ocean differently from the way I once did. One night I dreamt the sea was invisible and I could see every fish for miles, hanging as if in mid-air. When I woke up, I realized the dream revealed something breathtakingly obvious, but crucially important: you can't catch fish where there are none. When you consider there are very few fish in the sea and that winter chinook are almost always caught in exactly the same place, it becomes clear that visualizing the ocean in three dimensions is one step on the road to consistently catching them. To make an analogy, the chances of catching a fish without figuring out where they are are as slim as closing your eyes and shooting a rifle, expecting to bag a duck. Since my illumination I have always visualized the structure beneath me in three dimensions, using charts and depth sounder information.

Today we are fishing over uneven, rocky terrain on the edge of a channel 25 miles wide and 1,000 feet deep. Chinook almost invariably reside in relation to some bottom structure — a reef, a spire, a depression in a mud bottom. Only a tiny fraction of the space we glide across contains fish.

As the boat drags its Coyote, its Dragon Boat hootchie, let down 135 feet, I imagine the bottom below, the bottom on both sides, as well as in front of the boat. To our port we have excitement — rock ledges 100 feet down, bearing off with the shore in a roundness at ease with the moon. To our starboard, mud levels down to 250 feet. It is a mountain range come calming into a broad flat country of probability.

The sun burns ice into runoff and the dodger comes free. We have been trailing these so-called killers and neither diligence nor money has been rewarded. Then I see that in our going forward into the ocean we are slipping backward against the land. Unseen tide moves with the face of the moon and the boat loses ground. In fact, by motoring against the current, we are going nearly nowhere. "Why do veiny-eyed cormorants line up like accountants in fatal January," I say and point to the Jurassic, yellow-circled eyes on rocks bathed in gristling sea.

Now is the time to add the other dimensions. Most long-time fisher persons, i.e., those who perfect the basics and catch the salmon, will tell you that keeping in contact with the fish is probably the most important piece of strategy of all. We're certainly not in contact with the fish. Patrick's sucked back a lot of cigarettes and I've pontificated a lot of theory — good, solid, fish-catching stuff that isn't working at all. So I abandon the advice we've been given and fall back on plan B: moseying with the tide, checking out the back eddies en route to the island where I would have started had I not received advice.

We pick up speed going through the race, an area of five- and six- knot currents, brace ourselves in the three-foot chop that motors through island squeeze points. The sea roars above the engine. Sea lions we smell before we can see them. Strange how they will bask in their own excrement on rocks sensual as winter skin. Pigs in shit, they wait for an angler to get a fish on the line. Then they drag themselves on their elbows, flop from the wave-whiskered rock and vacuum off the salmon.

Time to admit the Coyote can't outsmart an animal with a thumb-tack brain, that the Dragon Boat plastic will go untouched until the pinks of summer light up the summer dreams of even the novice of the novice fishers. Plan B includes two or three other lures, none mentioned by the marina, all winter standbys that stud my records with fish. I pull out the trusty Mint Tulip, the Glow Below and Clover Leaf hootchies.

The sea swirls us in a broad arc through canyons of underwater rock. It plummets toward itself so fast the sea runs down into the trough of the Pacific Ocean. Two spins through the back end of these nameless rocks and I see why the sea lions lie in the thin winter rays: there are no fish for miles.

The tide roars through the passage, scouring the seabed, blowing bait and salmon before it. Think of tide as great wind that beats the underwater ridges, mountains and valleys as it would the desert. Nothing withstands the sea. I motor across a spire of rock that rises from 165 to 36 feet. Our lures pull along the underwater street to mudbanks of needlefish like clouds in winter valleys. The downrigger jiggles and when I reel in a turn, the shaking stops, indicating it has been rubbing a mud bottom, not catching a fish. I'm running out of tricks.

"Sometimes when I'm out here looking at all this fishless ocean, I think about your poem. The raven who flew straight for the curve of the ocean, out of sight of land, and it's flying to certain death."

Patrick's eyes turn into his mind and he checks his memory. "I don't remember that one."

A common misconception, I think. I expect a writer to know everything he's ever written, though it's hardly possible with someone who's written 20 books. We are approaching the island where I had intended to fish. Inexplicably it bears the name Church Rock, a rock in the broken-wave sea, wilderness in which a cupola would get blown to pieces.

Now I remember the fifth dimension: time. After visualizing how the bottom goes, and how it is hurried by the next dimension, water, there is one more shift and that is tide, when seamlessly the sea turns, on a journey to nowhere distinct. Our quarry takes his meals sometimes at dawn, but more often before the highest water and behind the lowest tide, and less often two hours before the black time of no sun. And winter chinook oblige; if you've been out too late, and feel as the raven flying resolutely to death, take heart — the fish will be looking for you in the middle of the day. They will be looking for you where the living is easy. They will be looking because they are winter feeders and this means they are looking for food even, as now, when the tide is not changing.

The tide has been dropping for four hours and should have pushed the salmon into the large pool behind Church Rock and toward The Bedfords. Two reefs poke up, providing calm for the current to deposit its catch. We hit our first fish on the first reef, an eight-pound chinook, a beautiful purple tinge to its winter colours.

We turn through the rip and come round again. Another chinook on the Clover Leaf. We now spend our time wisely, going in circles, five miles from where the gurus opined we should let down our gear. We have found the fifth dimension: time.

There is a song in the nerves of things. It is lightning in flesh. The club I raise and death snaps along their bodies. Corpses in the fish bucket, blood on the legs of our pants.

We are in the right spot, using the right thing, at the right time. We have, as the old-timers say, made contact. It has taken the time of the morning, a range of lures, and the bites have been received. And there are more to be caught, another theory to be tested. I have found it hard to believe that a flasher attracts fish by the light it reflects; at depth there should be no light. So I strip the tape from a flasher and send down a second Clover Leaf to 140 feet. Both of the last two keepers grab a mouthful of this line, which gives me something new to think about: when fishing deep, it may well be the action of the lure rather than the flash that matters, an observation not in keeping with the generally accepted doctrine of flashers.

After five hours of thermos coffee we relieve ourselves off the back. The stern lifts on a swell and I realize I'd look pretty bad in literary circles if I proved to be the one who killed the best poet in the country. I tell him he'd only survive an hour in the sea and perhaps I should tie him in. Maybe we'd catch a few more.

"Who knows, Dennis, four fish ain't bad," he says from beneath his old sailor-style cap. I wipe my thighs. My hands look out at you, ask the question: what does it take for men to be friends?

Idling back to Pedder Bay, the boat chooses its path, a horse, reins upon its withers. Feet propped against the hold, Patrick adds, "You haven't been that bad at finding me these fish, how about finding that poem?"

Again there is the heron frozen into the shoreline. There are the taps refusing to give their water. Other fishers kick salt off the dock, hands as empty as before.

The following poem resulted from the day Patrick and I fished. I was fortunate to win the Bliss Carman Award's silver medal.

The Hunger

Is there a benign mythology of colour that accounts for all this ice?
Take that blue boat in the blue distance where sea and sky become
each other. I am in that boat and I'm not blue.

Our talk, for now I've written two of us, is of the coyote spoon and
its green glow eye, the clover leaf, mint tulip, the hootchie let down.

Seamlessly the sea turns, landscape on a journey to nowhere distinct.
It pulls us through the back of ourselves and the Race in a roundness
at ease with the moon.

Our talk, when it comes again, is of the lost poem, the raven who
flew straight for the curve of the earth, the Pacific, and could not be
reconciled it was a water too far;

of the disease of creativity; the cheery probability one in five of poets
will kill themselves. What gives January the right to make skeletons
of everything?

Graham Green, for instance, burning for roulette. He pulled the trigger
in his ear and quenched a winning with alcohol. Pointless, for desire
is liquid too and falls toward the mind, the hand.

                                    To what weakness
does one lean willingly? The white powder rising to the pleasure centre
of the brain is poetry.

And before that rush the other rush when blood worms in the fit saying, "I love you." Why oh why do veiny-eyed cormorants line up like accountants in fatal January?

I wipe my thighs. My hands look out at you, ask the question: what does it take for men to be friends? There is a song in the nerves of things. It is lightning in flesh.

The club I raise and death snaps along their bodies. Corpses in the fish bucket, blood on the legs of our pants.

How islands bathe in the gristling sea, sensual as rounds of winter skin. On the rocks Jurassic, yellow-circled eyes. Cormorants snout the air for death and shiver in all their shabby hunger.

Idling back to Pedder, the boat chooses its path, a horse, reins upon its withers, haunches shifting like women. The harbour rips open like the bones of pregnant animals.

Again there is the flesh-starved heron frozen into the shoreline, the wild pathetic beauty we are all in.

What have I forgotten?   Be at peace, white heart.
Go easy, blood upon your knees.

Rainy Bay Winter Chinook

In 1787 Captain Charles Barkley sailed into Barkley Sound in his 400-ton, 20-gun vessel, the *Imperial Eagle,* with the intent of establishing a permanent trading link for England. As Captain James Cook had "claimed" the entire coast for England in 1778, Barkley's mission was largely to keep the Spanish from scooping the new territory and its abundant supply of sea otter pelts. Had Barkley been unsuccessful, the conflicting imperialistic ambitions of the two nations might have been inflamed. Spain and England were close to war — that era's version of a world war — and British Columbia would be a Spanish-speaking nation today if Spain had been the victor.

Instead of war, trade links with the then-23 Nootka Indian Tribes (known today as the Nuu-Chah-Nulth First Nations) were established for otter, fur seal, dogfish oil and wood spars. By 1859 when William Eddy Banfield, a carpenter from the HMS *Constance,* was installed as government agent, his census revealed eight distinct tribes in Barkley Sound alone.

Banfield, whose name was later modified to serve as the town of Bamfield's current descriptor, witnessed abundant saltwater resources. So rich were the protected Barkley Sound waters that aboriginals bent down the trees at the water's edge for herring to spawn on. The eggs were later dried and served as a delicacy at Klo-quan-na wolf initiation rites. So prodigious was the herring supply that Bamfield Harbour turned white with the release of milt.

As all fisher people will know, the gathering of ripening herring marks an occasion of great winter anticipation. This is because they become the focus of predatory interest for winter-feeder chinook. These are immature two-, three- and sometimes four-year-old spring salmon that, unlike other salmonids, may spend their winters feeding on local herring supplies in the protected inlets and inside waters close to shore rather than migrating to the open Pacific Ocean.

From just above legal length limits early in the season to as high as 30 pounds in late winter, these fish armies sweep around Vancouver Island and into Georgia Strait. In the time of Banfield, the then Ohiaht tribe (known today as the Huu-Ay-Aht First Nation) set out in their one-piece dugout canoes with lines of beaten and braided cedar bark. To these they tied vertebrae embedded in flesh to serve as lures, reeling in chinook that followed the herring into Vernon and Rainy bays.

They fished in the night or, prevented by taboo, took chinook only before noon. The nighttime ocean reflected long wood poles with Douglas-fir pitch set ablaze. In those days, the ocean was so abundant that chinook would rise to look at the light and thus be a target for a three-pronged spear if the meated hook was ignored. Made completely of wood and bone, the three prongs had hooks on their inside, resulting in a fish imprisoned within the striking end of the spear.

A century and a half later, knowledgeable anglers wait out the November gales, knowing that winter springs are not called feeders without reason. Winter presents the most consistent salmon fishing of the year. The fish may not be as large, averaging 5 to 15 pounds; however, they are actively feeding and putting on weight every day, unlike their hormonally challenged older brethren who, on their spawning runs in a few months time, become more and more fussy as the sun lengthens into its red end light of September.

Although the herring numbers are not as staggering as they once were, Barkley Sound still attracts huge schools of this prime salmon food. In 1998, for example, an aboriginal seine fleet drew a bead on 19,000 tons of the tiny squirmers. And this means that Barkley Sound is home to a brilliant winter fishery that far too few anglers treat themselves to when snow piles up in their driveways and minds like a kind of forgetfulness.

This is a pity because there are hotels and launching ramps and guides in all three towns rimming Barkley Sound. Vernon Bay is 30 minutes from Ucluelet, an aboriginal name meaning "people with a safe harbour." Anyone who has lurched through the potato patch of Amphitrite Point into this safe, deep indentation can understand why the name applies. Bamfield is less than a half hour's cruise through island passages. Port Alberni, originally named by the Spanish in 1789 after the captain of military forces at Nootka Sound, lies 50 minutes up the inlet of the same name.

The winter fishery owes its sterling qualities to the herring and to the fact that Barkley Sound is relatively remote from large urban centres such as Victoria. As top of the piscine food chain, as carnivores, chinook need the extra body weight and oil during winter when the surrounding ocean water may be as low as six to eight degrees Celsius. Accordingly, they stay in close contact with their prey. Any chinook moseying by will automatically stop and take up residence. As winter progresses, the number of chinook increases; they come but they do not leave.

Anglers arriving on Barkley Sound shores will find the other conditions necessary for winter success: calm water and relatively slow tidal currents. The former suits the angler and the latter suits both angler and fish; chinook do not favour bucking currents and fishing gear works far better in slower water than in fast.

Rainy Bay and, particularly, Vernon Bay provide slow-moving, deep water close to shore. Ancestors of the Huu-Ay-Aht and Uchucklesaht gathered herring spawn here for thousands of years, and beneath their cedar boats lay the same structure that still draws the chinook today. Of the five salmon species, chinook is the most resolutely structure related — in this case, rock ledges under the water along with several sharp points, in the lee of which the bait and salmon hold. The deep, fjord-like conditions prevalent at the head of a sound, i.e., a land indentation open to surging tidal current at only one end, makes for a perfect place to fish in winter months.

Unlike inland areas where, from December to March, local anglers shovel snow from walks and reflect, sadly but sagely, that a fly landed on an ice-coated lake just isn't going to receive a strike, Barkley Sound towns are shovelling out from under the latest drift from cherry trees. In earliest January, pink dusky blooms with stamens like eyelashes begin to drift earthward. By March it is a torrent and locals can be seen sweating as they dig out from under nature's first sloughing of detritus.

There is no need to be annoyed at such lucky individuals: forsake your shovel and head for the flowers. On most misty days the tooth-like ridges blend in the background and the GPS picks up the Broken Island and Deer Group islands before you see them. Upon arrival you will probably find yourself the only boat on the bay.

After the bracing, car-challenging trip down the Nitinat Main and a night in the tourist-depleted, pretty town that is Bamfield, I leave at dawn for the run down Trevor Channel. First, though, a quick dash around Aguilar Point to take in, once again, the 20-storey rock, known from Indian legend as Execution Rock. In a previous summer's troll, I had looked up at the impressive height with its stain of iron oxide on one side and the cavern of softer rock the ocean has licked so long that a shaft runs right through to shore. My guide told me that it received its name from the English marching the Indians off into bone splinters. Below, of course, black basalt rock would make quick work of the unfortunate.

Other than a quick revulsion, I would have forgotten this silent reminder of a former massacre, but someone else in the town told me, "No, it wasn't the English, it was the Spanish. But they were marching the English off the rock. That's why there was almost a world war here." Then I was told that it wasn't the way I'd heard it second, it was: "The English shoved the Spanish off the rock." Then I became interested and decided to spend some time in the dusty, mouldy provincial museum trying to verify the story.

What I uncovered, however, was yet another story: the rock, known as Kee-hin, was a typical Indian stronghold, intended to prevent attack from miffed neighbours. Unfortunately, due to dancing young men into adulthood on its peak, the Ohiaht were taken by surprise by Clallam tribesmen, who rowed the 90 miles across the open Juan de Fuca Strait to avenge the murders of the chief's sons. The Clallam murdered all the resident Indians on a night without a moon as foretold in the legend of the sacrifice by a former ruler said to have ruled 300 years.

So, I had four stories, none of which were the same, and the question *what is true?* subsequently led me to write two historical novels set on Barkley Sound and the Broken Island group. The first sentence of the first expresses the point of stories, whether written, spoken or unuttered: "Who is there among us who knows what is true in the words that are spoken and the words that are set down?"

So the sound has occupied a large part of my creative thinking for more than half a decade. And I have come to know more than I would have expected, about its history, and about how even the written word is fallible, representing only the view of the author, just as the spoken word is, in a tradition from the mouth.

Before the winter fishing, I also detour through Robbers Passage for a haunting view of the former Greenpeace vessel, the *Sea Shepherd*. Some years ago its Picasso-rendered white-dove fo'c's'le was abandoned in Ucluelet. A fire followed, reducing the proud vessel to a hulk that was sold by the harbour authority for a humbling loonie. For posterity, I strip a piece of rust the size of my hand and can't help but feel disappointed with Greenpeace for abandoning this former symbol of life and unspoiled nature.

I put the chunk in a freezer-lock bag and motor past Diplock Island and then Baeria Rocks, heading for the fog-laden Effingham shore. Throttling back the Volvo engine (with its throaty reliability that every long-term boat owner knows is the unmistakable sound of money), I begin in the deep water to let out lines.

The purpose in this strategy is to locate the bait in one tack. The depth sounder lights up with bait 400 feet wide and 200 feet deep. So thick are the herring that the sounder cannot penetrate them to read bottom. Morning rain pings on the canvas and runs in streams to the gunwales. Around us, the water is so quiet that raindrops hit and bounce off the water like steel pellets, and there is the small sound of effervescence. Like Pavlov's dogs, long-time anglers salivate at that sound; it is the release of air from tens of thousands of tiny swim bladders touching the surface.

Barkley Sound in winter is a plug, hootchie and, above all else, bait domain. The Tomic 602, a solid open-ocean favourite, finds consistent use here. In hootchies, blend lighter colours with glow-in-the-dark properties — for example, the Glow Below. As an alternative, keep a blue-and-silver needlefish on a 36-inch leader. As with other feeder fisheries, these chinook are deeper than summer fish. One hundred twenty to 140 feet is the witching depth.

Successful Bamfield guides employ a bait set-up that appears to have come from some chalice in the tomb of Tutankhamen. "Nearly mummified" does little to describe the leather-like appearance of these salt-sucked herring. The tight spiral desired is obtained by drilling a second hole in the teaserhead closer to the centre line. Thus mounted, the desiccated herring truly spins like a bullet released from its barrel.

Off Effingham it comes back to me that the next bay over is the historical home of the Toquaht First Nation (earlier Toquart). Banfield's 1860 census of the tribes from Port Renfrew through to Tofino revealed a few of very low numbers. Among them, the Toquart had only 11 men remaining, due in large part to good fortune — they had been away. It was Indian custom, when desiring new territory or fulfilling a revenge, that every single person was killed. This included the elderly, all women, children and babies, with perhaps a few comely girls saved for slaves and bringing forth of children for the conquering tribe. The Ohiaht word for children is *wick-tuck-yu,* and translates most directly as totally ignorant and worthless persons.

A century and a half later, prodigious schools of herring return in the mixing month of March. And today, anglers prone to bolt from their chair when the rod moves an angstrom have to learn to keep their cool. The top end of the sound fills with so much bait that rods regularly receive asymmetric jolts — usually the sign of fish — one after the other. In years past and years to come this pattern still results from the line hitting herring as it moves through the tightly bunched schools.

Prior to the time of Charles Barkley, the Ohiaht aboriginals who dominated the cultural history of Barkley Sound called the herring *kloos-mit* and the winter spring *tso-hah.* They believed that the fish was a man in a fish's body. As mentioned, certain sanctions applied to the catching of the chief of all fishes. Winter feeders were not to be caught in the decline of the sun, nor were their entrails to be left in the water or on the beach. Otherwise the whole tribe of spring salmon would emigrate. There was conservation purpose in those beliefs — Barkley Sound salmon and herring remain in great numbers for the angler of the third millennium.

Swiftsure Elephants

Sun lifts from sea so still a twoonie would roll to Neah Bay on the American side of Juan de Fuca Strait. Peter Hovey spreads the substantial bushy tips of his moustache with thumb and index finger and offers a metal card from which he would push a pill or two into my hand. "Care for a Gravol, Dennis?"

Something's wrong here. The sea lies at my feet like liquid cloth and the sky is an endless blue promise. There is no malevolence, no hint of trouble, no smidgeon of doubt in this new August morning. But I know better. When a guide pops back motion-sickness medicine, it's time for the fisher to load up, too. I knock back Gatorade and pills as we inscribe an arc past Thrasher Bay where 8,000 campers a year set out on the 50-mile trek of a lifetime, known around the world now as the West Coast Trail. The trail used to be for saving lives of passengers and crew from ships foundered on the black, basalt coastline of Vancouver Island. Those hundreds of boats included many, like the

Valencia, that turned into the strait in a southeast storm under sail and, with a conflicting flood tide, were pushed 60 miles off course to end in disaster in the plowing surf and rocks.

Half an hour later, the Carmanah lighthouse bleeps its solitary warning eye from a Turneresque painting of gold that grows from mist and lays summer on our arms. We turn offshore into a sea of steel and ride the swell, wave to wave, like the backs of huge unconscious animals the size of city blocks. To starboard, killer whales blow into morning, sequential as chessmen, lifting tons of black and white into the sky — the ease and indifference of wilderness.

Shore is soon lost. Fog closes like a wrapper. The sea is a feeling in the stomach, as we plane troughs deeper than the boat. The GPS gleams the runway-like road we travel to our destination: the three cloverleaf-shaped, underwater reefs known as Swiftsure Bank, 15 miles west of Port Renfrew and then 15 miles south from Carmanah into the open Pacific Ocean. The GPS marks the location of the Chicken Ranch, as the halibut spot is known; these are usually the edges of flats or canyons that halibut migrate onto in May from as far as 1,500 miles away and from winter depths of a mile. These fish of the bad breath and mixed-up eyes (the left eye migrates toward the right in the first few months of life) come to their summer residences on gravel heaps, where they sort themselves out by size.

When the GPS beeps, Peter nods his head and dons his shades. With a cowboy hat, he looks more like Richard Petty, the NASCAR driver, than Petty himself. He braces himself between captain's chair and gunwale as though the seas in chop around and over us are non-existent. "Time to get the fat ones." I look out into elephant hills spilling their crowns. They lumber toward us. Water washes the deck of his 21-foot Robalo and we stand in it up to our ankles. I think he's got to be kidding but am unwilling to voice my opinion lest I be thought a chicken. After all, I am supposed to be a great white hunter because I write about fishing.

I am handed a stout white rod with an orange glowhead octopus hootchie bib and one-pound weight. While it free-falls to the bottom, I wedge my feet into crevices to keep from falling overboard. One thunk on the bottom 230 feet below and the short thick rod heads for the water. I've got a sandwich in my mouth, the rod propped in my belt and Peter by my side, brandishing a gaff like Captain Hook. My theory on fishing is this: the greater the unlikelihood of your getting to the rod the greater the likelihood you will get a bite. This I call the theory of being compromised. Stated another way: the more compromised you are the greater your chance of getting a bite. So I suggest to those with whom I fish that they open a pop, pour some coffee, put a sandwich in their mouths, light a cigar and open the zipper of their pants.

The rod wows, under the galloping run of halibut. Drool begins to slide from my mouth down my chin and my sandwich opens the other side and begins dropping lettuce and tomato and mayonnaise and tuna (we are fishing, after all) all over me. In the case of halibut, this phase goes on and on and on.

When the barn door finally hits the surface, Peter pokes it with a truncheon. "To settle it down, my boy," he says, cigarette chomped firmly between his teeth. "I call this an attitude adjuster. He'll be happier soon." Without ceremony, he hauls up and over the gunwale, then down into the open-mouthed fishbox in the deck.

Then he takes the raw seawater hose and washes the slime from the deck. "To keep us from falling out, my friend." Radar on the dash continues greenly sweeping its eye on a world we cannot see. White-knuckling the steering wheel in one hand and throttle in the other, Peter turns into the seas and launches us back to the GPS mark. We've already drifted half a mile. This is the Pacific; 6,000 feet of water rises up from the sea and plumes over the bank into Juan de Fuca Strait. "Heck, on a calm day, the swells reach 10 or 12 feet. It's bracing, my man."

Holding onto one of the six handholds strategically mounted around the boat, I look to the horizon and realize, as we fall from the back of one huge wave into the valley below, that I don't have a clue where we are. I have been turned around in the fog and have no idea where shore is. Good reason for a full array of electronics blinking away in soothing colour, our connection with the rest of mankind. I sometimes dream the dream of no compass. In that dream I turn to go home, and find (the dream does not come with my GPS as a possibility) the compass heads only east. If I turn to the west, it reads east. If I turn north or south, it reads east. And I am left to choose whatever direction I want and find, when my finite gas tanks run out, that I have, too bad, headed in the fog to Japan.

Continually checking the radar, Peter offers the offhand observation, "Freighters come out of the fog like skyscrapers. This is just swell." He points up to the wave. "They turn it into chop the size of houses." To me, this *does* look like houses. And the waves come from two directions; where their tops add up, they smack a geyser another floor into the sky.

The gaudy skirt free-falls to the bottom. Peter explains the current is so strong that the lure won't reach bottom if it gets behind the boat; line drag prevents it. To stay on top of the lure he shifts into reverse, and the engine backs us up and over the incoming swells. "I've buried the engine in waves before," he says and laughs.

I'm standing yanking on the pool-cue-thick fishin' pole and its "upside" levelwind reel, not finding his nonchalance reassuring, while he reaches over and harpoons a 50-pounder so hard the shaft bends sideways. The tip connects to a line and bumper. "I've seen the big gals zip a Scotchman out of sight 50 feet. Then you have to search around a while and find 'em in the hills." And the big halibut, all female, rise to more than 300 pounds.

The transom rides the next hump and my Gatorade pinwheels across the deck spewing itself. I scramble after it, and hook my next halibut hard. One foot on the bottle, apple in my teeth, the rod slips from my hip and up under my armpit. Peter plants a big thumb under the brim of his cowboy hat and offers a helpful mixture of derision and advice, "Well, missie, you gonna have a hard time lifting that butt." Picture Nick Nolte, standing in the bullets of *The Thin Red Line,* chewing out his men for being scared.

After my 15-minute struggle lifting a grand piano to the top, Peter takes the leader in his gloved hand. Foot against the hull he gaffs the halibut up and over and down into the fishbox again. He kicks the door shut and sluices the pitching deck. In his lure bucket are 10-inch scampi tails. Hooks are baited with chunks of octopus he keeps in a Tupperware container: scent, after the sound of thunking the bottom, is the key to luring the fish. The huge rubbery skirts flutter in the water. Surprisingly, since visual light doesn't go down much over 100 feet, colour is a key ingredient in catching halibut: chartreuse, red and black, yellow and green and orange. Find the right one, and everyone switches over.

Then, to my amazement, the sea goes absolutely calm. It bulges like a magnifying glass. "Slack tide, Den." Acres of bait erupt as far as I can see and seagulls plunder the sea. So close I can reach down and touch them, coho and mackerel swim by the boat. I've never seen anything like it — two species in the same school, and so green they have no fear of the boat.

"It's an amazing rearing ground, upwelling feeding plankton and bait. Thirty-seven kinds of rockfish." Peter points to the depth sounder and fish swim across the screen in patches from surface to bottom. "No one even fishes salmon out here, there's so many back at Owen Point. But look at them all."

When Peter does guide for salmon he fishes electric downriggers and has an ingenious system. His depth sounder marks the fish. Beside it he's rigged buttons so he can troll, looking at the depth sounder screen, and raise and lower his downriggers without leaving the captain's chair. "All I need is something to connect my auto helm to my depth sounder. When I set it on forward view, the boat will take itself to the fish!"

I switch to a light spinning reel with a red Deadly Dick and dangle the lure in the water beside the boat. And then the theory of being compromised: I bite into another tuna sandwich and in a silver instant, the rod pitches up and over the railing and were it not for my being beside it and catching the reel going out, it would have completed its journey into the sea, never to be seen again. The reel sings. The leader zings like a submarine antenna.

But the ocean is at work with the moon and the period of slack passes. The sea, like mounds of molten chocolate, begins to form. Mountains rise beside the boat. Peter whacks his dash-mounted GPS and shakes his head. Then he takes a hand-held GPS from his pocket and brings us to the mark. "Out here you gotta have backup equipment or you won't get back." The radar sweeps colour around its screen. Waves wash the decks and overwhelm the scuppers. Weather reels from the VHF.

Peter tells me big halibut are both territorial and mobile, so they're found in the same spot every time, every summer after moving onshore. He taps his GPS. "Catching fish by satellite. Can you beat that?"

Then terra firma 250 feet down and a wave lifting until the rod almost pulls me from the boat. "We lose the occasional client that way ... just a joke, Dennis, relax." Peter backs up one wave and down the next, but can't free the lure. I let out slack, the usual solution; still no luck.

"Holy shit," Peter says and points to the radar. He reefs line around a cleat and throws the throttle forward. Plastered against the outboard I watch the line snap free, look up the 50-foot wall of freighter materializing from the mist. We are 15 miles offshore and the pilot can't see the front of his own ship let alone the blip we make. Peter looks at me, at my white face, and slaps his knee. He leans into the throttle and the brim of his hat flattens to his forehead.

Soon we have left the bank and the freighter in the fog. Peter plugs numbers into his autohelm and swivels in his chair. He puts his cowboy boots on the dash, cracks a beer and flips his cell phone open. The boat quarters the following sea, a sideways ride we settle into. "Honey," he says into the tiny phone against his ear, "fire up the hali-pot. The boys are coming in with grub." The carnage? Eight halibut, zero elephants, one coho and one disturbingly humanoid ratfish.

The Long and Winding Way to Tofino

I am walking out of Lordco Parts Ltd. twiddling the new rotor inside my boat's distributor cap. In my last preparations for the ride to Tofino, I thought, as a long-time boater who understands that breakdowns can lead to being adrift without power, injury and, in the six- to eight-degree Celsius ocean, death in less than an hour, that picking up this and other items would provide a little insurance.

Then I'm thinking the rotor looks a teeny bit longer than the original. Hmm. And it occurs to me that if the rotor is too long, it will rip the distributor cap to pieces. Of course the most likely place I will install it is miles from anywhere on the straight-as-a-ruler coastline that runs from Victoria to Cape Beale near Bamfield, most of which is wave-bashed from the open Pacific Ocean. So I go back inside just to be sure and find that the rotor has three different versions and I've been given one that is, obviously, wrong.

Walking out the door with renewed confidence, I decide, nevertheless, to check this rotor on the engine, prior to pulling out. This is Sunday of the Labour Day weekend, and I am not going to find any store open on Monday. Back at the boat for the third time today, I find the new rotor works like a charm, in fact better than the current one, which developed a funny jiggly sound during use. I discover that the current rotor on which I was going to rely is deficient; its metal retention bar has fallen out. I'm glad to have found this problem, too, before casting lines. This is what 25 years of experience does for you: anticipate problems before they arise.

In fact, I began planning two months before pulling up stakes. I purchased a GPS and it took two months of driving all over town to figure out how it worked. Thank goodness I had not left it to chance, thinking I could learn the GPS on the trip. Without doubt there was no way I could have got proficient in time for it to be useful; that is, the most vital piece of equipment would have been non-functional. This is the kind of oversight that gives the shakes to boaters long in the tooth. I also attended to annual maintenance: new stainless fuel lines, new antenna for the radio, fuses, new battery, gas-line filters, and so on.

Then I boned up on chart and course. I covered the entire journey by purchasing all the charts and doing the course and fuel-consumption dead-reckoning thing. Which is to say that while my boat is rated at 8.5 gallons per hour, I felt safer assuming 10 gallons and its built-in margin as the basis for calculating fuel consumption. With 40 gallons in the tanks, I should be able to run at least four hours, i.e., about 80 miles, to somewhere along the Graveyard of the Pacific, with its couple of hundred wrecks, near Bonilla Point past Port Renfrew. Late in my planning, I was informed that refuelling was not to be trusted in Port Renfrew as it sometimes had gas and sometimes did not, and that the gas often had a high level of condensed water, something that stops my carburetor-challenged, V8, five-litre, 185-horsepower Volvo engine dead in its tracks. The thought of two hours of breaking down the engine while adrift in a rising onshore breeze did nothing to offer reassurance. Of course, I had long before added an in-line filter to aid the filter on the engine — and still broke down.

No. I would have to make it all the way to Bamfield from Victoria. To be on the safe side, I brought along 25 gallons of extra fuel in five jerry cans, expecting from them 2.5 hours of 20-knot planing. By Sunday evening, I had had to replace three that were not vapour safe — they would make the boat a bomb. The siphoned containers were stored in the bow along with groceries, fishing tackle, downriggers, bag of clothes and camera gear.

I go to sleep early and arrive at Oak Bay Marina at 4:30 AM. In the cool expectant darkness, the engine thrums up over Labour Day Monday, the slip of nylon from flags shrugging lazily on the quay, the clank of radar reflectors on sailboat masts.

With the slippery light of first sun colouring the sea metal and red, I round the golf course corner, Mouat Reef Marker and Enterprise Channel north of Trial Island, and set my GPS trail for Race Rocks perhaps 18 miles away. In the interval, to the north of me, the bright yellow Quarantine Buoy shines in thrown spotlight sun, then it falls behind the wake that falls behind the boat aimed for the Race. Five-thirty AM, half an hour out of port, and the zebra lighthouse cannot be seen. Instead, a wall of fog dense as forest. "Man," I think, "wiped out before I even start." I throttle back, deciding what to do, to admit defeat or go forward into fog, without radar. Now a fishing boat materializes and I take it as a shrouded omen; if he can get through, I can, too. It doesn't occur to me that his boat is on auto pilot and safe as can be. I just hit the gas, my overloaded boat struggles onto the plane and the two of us go boldly into the fog, my eyes glued to the compass.

At full speed inside the room of fog it seems that nothing else can exist, that sunlight cannot be, that rock and cliff have been erased. Then I am swerving among sport-fishing boats, risen too quick. I am on them, turn and spray their transoms, then pass in velocity back into the fog before they can raise a fist my way. Not very safe. I am pulling back on the throttle to avoid plowing into an island that has crept into my track. I break through the fog, and there is Becher Bay. I double-click the waypoint for Church Rock for my return trip. Then another double-click at Beechy Head where I pass wide to avoid an armada of 500 boats and swing into the silence and cool sweat of fog. It occurs to me that one must never take a waypoint, travel a curve and set a second. This will result in hitting the island on the way back. Three points need setting: before the island, beside and after.

Sun again on Secretary Island, then back into a finger of nothingness. So the morning goes: fog like an accordion on the southwest shore of Canada. In and out, double-clicking and naming. And growing concern, as the digital numbers sweep my stopwatch, to be off the water before noon; the daily convection wind builds giraffes off Owen Point, great beasts strolling the distant savannah. So I give the boat a little more juice and it responds by giving me one to one and a half knots more. And we appear and disappear as though fog extends a hand inland to grasp and hold where it can. Where it cannot, I find sun on my face, I find ocean black and at peace with itself.

A finger of fog at Jordan River. A finger of fog at Port Renfrew. The only two points I know between Victoria and Cape Beale. And I have relayed briefly the story of this coast that has taken many boats and more lives. The *Valencia*. Who could not feel sympathy for the men and women and children tied in the rigging so the ocean could not rip them free? The grainy black photo of white sea and bodies in the sway of masts. More than one hundred dead, many bodies smacked against rocks until unrecognizable. The *British Colonist* photo, ship foundering for days, captain's fingers blown by the line shot to shore. All within sight of the West Coast Life-Saving Trail near Pachena lighthouse.

And curiously, my fuel gauge seems not to be working. It registers less fuel than it should and hence it must be defective. Defective — or have I used more fuel than I figured? I am somewhere off the Indian settlements of Whyac and Clo-oose and the Nitinat Bar where log booms floated out 80 years ago. This rock bar in outflow tide against a storm makes for 20-foot cresters that kill people every year, even today.

After three hours I realize I have used four hours of fuel and there is a very real danger of running out. After all, and included in my estimate, a vessel must have fuel enough to almost make its intended port, and if a storm brews, enough to return to the last fuel dock passed — Sooke Basin is a long long way back.

It comes to me that I have varied from my pre-trip plans: by bumping planing speed a smidge over easy cruising speed, I have used 33 percent more fuel than intended. In addition, the portable tanks have helped push the bow down, the extra weight effectively reducing cruising distance by making the engine push more water. I pull the throttle to zero, and swirl within the fog. I hold jerry can after jerry can wobbly and heavy over the gunwale and make the spout hit the filler hole, spilling much. This chore would be impossible in weather. Today, I ride glassy water in the middle of fog as though nothing exists in the world but me and my fuel problems.

The purpose in speeding up was to get me off the water sooner on this exposed, wilderness shore. I estimated fuel consumption to give a cruising distance of 130 to 153 miles. Bamfield is 88 to 92 nautical miles, so I felt confident. But now, having burned an extra hour's fuel, my range is cut down to 110 to 130 miles. I still have wriggle room, but heavy seas off Cape Beale, all the way from the Orient, would present a hell of an obstacle due to the need to wallow — that is cross the valleys and crests of the waves and hope no breakers bear down on me. What I expect is a typical, fine, late-summer afternoon with its typical eight-foot seas.

I do not have the luxury of making revised calculations. At the same time, I feel past the point of going back to Port Renfrew. That would offer shelter but not reliable fuel. Before me more fingers of fog and about two hours to my intended port of Bamfield. The jerry cans held two and a half hours of fuel and there is what remains in the tanks — too slim for my comfort. It surfaces in my mind that in the late 1800s, the mail and provisions trip was five days by dugout canoe, and that once, they brought, improbably, a stand-up piano lashed between the thwarts.

Closer to Bonilla Point, looking into the distance, out beyond to Seabird Rocks I see the breeze springing four-foot waves pitching into white directly at me. When I reach them my speed must be reduced to just below planing. This is the highest consumption stage, even more than speeds above cruising.

Rounding Beale, the cape named for the purser of Captain Barkley's 1787 crew, I can still see the remains of a boat among the rocks, wedged into a crevice upside down. It was reduced from a vessel 40 feet long on Christmas Eve a few years past to a remnant 18 inches high by the pounding it received, and little hope for the members who remained in the water. Two died, two survived; one of the saved strode from the white foam sea, the other had refused to put a foot beyond Sooke Basin and was let off hours before.

I am alone, slopping and broaching the crests and troughs, thrown left and right by chop. But it is a leniency of water that when it turns with you, fear is replaced by exhilaration, the slewing on the crest until you catch the speed of the ride and move so fast a deep V-hull breaks the green sea valley into white bookends. I will arrive.

I round Aguilar Point, the entrance to the harbour and the pretty inlet that divides east Bamfield from west Bamfield. The only crossing is by water taxi or one's own boat. During school season children are picked up in their raincoats and rubbers and, with bright orange safety vests, ferried on the yellow boat across to the landing where, up the hill and into the forest, is the school.

Francis Mawson Rattenbury designed the original French chateau on the top of the hill where, below it, stands the concrete Transpacific Cable Station, also of his design. Rattenbury blasted the stone face of the cliff and made the fragments into concrete. The chateau was burned in the 1960s but the concrete building is now the property of five universities and is used for marine research. Once it was the busiest hotspot of information relayed across the Pacific by underwater cable and on to Churchill in England for the war against Adolph Hitler.

So much history, so much of man and all that, is forgotten. I am cognizant of my smallness, in my blue chair in my blue boat with my orange life vest beneath me. Moving out at daybreak, into the mist-enclosed Broken Islands, I make passage between Helby and Sandford islands into Imperial Eagle Channel where residual swell rolls like water asleep, glass walls green, and in between these, on a crest, a fleet of trollers, hog lines out, taking their share of coho destined for the Stamp River. The Deer Group, the Broken Islands Group wait patiently in the rain, waiting for nothing, really, but waiting just the same. Above their lines of white sand, cliffs and trees with broken heads from too many years in the wind.

A chart makes these islands domestic, flattens them, lets us look down upon their shapes. On the water they look anything but what they should. Charts don't show how high the trees, and in the off-yellow representations in the open papers a sea person takes to sea the topographical nature of the islands leaves much to be desired. They are shoved together to the horizon and their layers begin and end in haze. I pay much attention to the chart and making the islands in here, on this blue numbered chart, look like the islands out there. West coast rain, its endless voice. The sound of drops hitting incoming swell, and being reduced to perfectly round droplets until they too succumb to the sea. Yes, rain is a constant companion and I am an intruder in a vegetative making of love. Rainforest, jungle, mist, the seething green.

I know that once a mistake is made, every other direction is also mistaken. In fog, I once ended up in the United States on my way to Oak Bay, leaving me next to nothing in fuel for the return across the Haro Strait line. So I move hesitantly through the white-log islands, skirt well-browned, kelp-bed aprons. I disregard the fir-doubled basalt, making sure I can place each island among its cohorts, checking until I am certain.

And finally, the steep shore at the back-door passage to Ucluelet. Here, *circa* 1904, perhaps the coast's greatest unknown diary was written. Surely the match for or greater than the well-known one of Father Brabant at Ahousaht, it was written by Ucluelet's Presbyterian minister, Melvin Swartout, under the pen name Haicks.

The high rock face at harbour's entrance is again typical of easily defended Indian refuges on the west coast. A braiding of kelp across the channel gave warning of the arrival of hostile canoes, come to kill and take slaves. Into the empty marina I come, and when the boat slides around its corner, I chunk it into reverse and the stern pulls to the slip and stops. All night, the eagle that rose from the rock, from its nest like an upturned hand, flies through my mind and when it lands it is the day I awake.

Past Amphitrite Point I move with local fishermen out into the slop left over from 14-foot waves the day before. These steep, brittle, uncresting waves of 5 and 6 feet launch my 21-foot, 1-ton boat so clear of the water the leg and propeller can be seen. At the top of that arc, my gasoline cans, my tackle, my bedding and clothes fly in an instant of free fall around me in some weird version of weightlessness training for astronauts. At the end of my flight I hit so hard the boat compresses on the diagonal, ejecting the door to my cabin from its tracks. Had there not been a full enclosure, a camper-style canvas on the back, the door would have flown into the sea never to have my eyes on it again.

What I do not yet know is this: the front hatch has ripped out its hinges. If I plow into only one of the thousands of waves I will cross today, the boat will be lost and I along with it. This is the continental shelf off Pacific Rim National Park. People from all over the world come to watch infinity fall on the sand and run its tables up to an assortment of pink little toes. Serene, beautiful, yes, but for me, moving into fog, very dangerous indeed.

I find that where I switch from one chart to another there is a gap and then a change in scale in the second chart. Foolish of me not to notice this because in fog, one has no idea where one is or where one is going. So I motor along, within view of the shore and the crashing of its waves upon the white sand.

The fog descends, the thin slice of visibility narrows. It pulls colour from the sky. Taking my bearing here I turn right to enter the channel for Tofino only to pull back the throttle when I see clamshells on the bottom and hear the depth sounder ring a grazing with death. Now I am sure I am lost and do not know whether I have even, in the fog, passed right by the entrance to Tofino and am motoring up the west coast until I run out of gas.

Immediately, coming from the bay I later find is named Coxswain, I lift over eight-foot glassy walls of water. Crossing the sea come and come for me, one second fog is all I see, and the next is only water.

Lost on the west coast, I motor into the next false channel and am about to turn and head back the hours along the strung starpoints of my GPS when the ghzzz of an engine can be heard. In the gap between islands, a 15-foot, centre-console fibreglass runabout travels the line between sea and sky. Saved at the last second. If he can come out, then I can go in; it must be the channel to Tofino. I swing around the outer shore. Green sucks white down the rocks.

By now the runabout has disappeared and I, moving by compass, point my boat down the channel from which he came. Soon something darker behind the grey. Then the suddenness of rock and kelp, and my hand that rides the throttle always, pulls back and the boat skids to a stop. Backing my way out of the kelp, I assess where I am, knowing from the charts there are three islands that mark the shallow entrance.

"The first should be right there," I say, as it becomes so in front of me, and then the next. I tap my way as with a cane and hug the shore of buildings. I know the floats where I will end, and that the tide will be steaming by. Tofino is one of the few places on B.C.'s coast where tide smokes through the harbour. One had better handle the boat with authority. No time for hesitance, motor right to the dock, hit reverse and out to tie off the stern. The flood rushes seaweed and flotsam, small fish that it catches.

On the dock, all lines and spring lines down, bumpers between boat and dock, I sit a while and feel the warm come all the way, eight minutes in flight from the sun that makes our lives possible. My hand still bears the impression of the wheel I held the many hours. And then I get to the task of taking the door apart. There is no other solution, the boat having flexed from the bow back until it threw the door from its track — something I don't have the long arms and the muscles to match. So the cabin's walk-through window is flipped forward to allow access to the deck-mounted ½-inch Plexiglas hatch. It is here, in the first sunlight in my day and with safety in abundance, that I notice the clasp and padlock have ripped out of material I couldn't break with a sledge hammer. As I lift the Plexiglas, it comes away in my hand. Both hinges have also broken, from hitting a wave 10,000 waves ago on this long September transit. Stainless steel hinges, stainless steel screws, snapped off and out as simply as twigs.

No words come out of my mouth as I stand there, fingers and thumbs hanging by my sides. I don't know what to think. Any wave after the break, any wave in the many hours until Tofino could have, if I had taken a "green one," ripped out the hatch, filled the boat with a ton of water and killed the engine. The next wave would have turned me broadside to the endless glass doors peaking my way and the third would have rolled the boat and me to being dead. I pull my tin box of tools from the bow. The Robertson screwdriver moves like a backward clock. Screws make the sound of small metal in the tin tray. Perhaps fortune favours the bold; perhaps those with 25 years of smacking into waves. Not many times do you walk away from death.

In the coming sun next morning, I am up by 5:30, yawning into the first orange tentacles crossing Earth. An island of sleeping mountains, very old, round teeth. Though the west is calm completely, I know that with the day, it will claim the land and water and make them so they cannot be told apart.

Fishing for Dreams

Most anglers spend their entire fishing careers plying home territory while dreaming of a pilgrimage to one of British Columbia's fishing meccas. Along with Langara Island and Rivers Inlet, Hakai Pass is one of the holy-trinity destinations. Two hundred fifty miles north of Vancouver's South Terminal, Hakai is an immense float-plane-access fishery with hundreds of surf-plowed rocky points and heat-creased basaltic promontories dotting the 360,000-acre Hakai Recreational Park.

My advice to the true believer is this: make a plan today. Save those loonies and twoonies. You owe it to yourself to crusade your way to Hakai Pass Beach Resort and transform your fishing dreams into reality. You can sell the idea to your spouse on the grounds you aren't just spending hard-earned currency on your own fun. The first alternative is to suggest your partner come along. If he or she agrees, then you go. Of course, the one little problem becomes two, i.e., paying for two people rather than only one. If your partner doesn't want to come, get in touch with me. (Sorry, I couldn't help that.) Simply point out that all the salmon, halibut and googly-eyed red snapper you return with — of course in prime condition, filleted, blast-frozen and vacuum-packed — would cost so much in the store that you will have completely paid for the trip by the time you get home.

Over the past two decades resorts have come a long way and now put together finely honed, remote-location board and room. Today, most offer all-inclusive fishing packages. The expression means just that: chef-prepared meals, with special plates for the allergy-challenged among us; thoroughly contemporary or period rooms; fish-till-you-drop guiding; snazzy, 12.5-foot Sage rods matched with special edition Islander reels (you'll be tempted to purloin them); a handsome fleet of boats using zero-fume four strokes; and often, an open bar, including selected wines for meals. Sometimes families come along, intending to watch the endless surf of West Beach, survey the sea lion haulouts and view the islands like long sleeping animals, and even the most blasé turns into a fisherperson.

By the time my plane skids to a halt, summer has already offered forth chinook to 52 pounds, halibut to 140, coho to 24 and ling cod to 41. We are introduced to the guides as our feet hit the floats. All guides have nicknames and this is one of the interesting parts of remote trips: learning the "handles" used on VHFs and the stories behind them. Ernie "Mad Dog" Webb (rumour has it that this very mild, generous and thoroughly competent guide bares his chompers if chow isn't in the dish when his seat hits the chair) takes me down to the dock and shows me how to rig his version of the locally named Hakai Hammer. He feels that chinook want a slower bait presentation, one that allows for a lot of variation, in the method of motor-mooching brought to classic perfection in the Hakai area.

Ernie's version of a cutplug is a thing of beauty, and as an angler who is a student of the game, I appreciate when other fishermen demonstrate their skill and knowledge, developed over the decades of their fishing careers. Ernie uses red Gamakatsu hooks rigged in a double sliding-hook arrangement on a 6-foot, 25-pound-test leader attached with a Palomar knot to a simple swivel. His bait preparation is critical. He slices whole, semi-frozen herring perpendicular to the dorsal surface behind the gill plate in a single slice with a cut-your-hand-off-sharp knife. In the same slice, he adds a 30-degree bevel from one lateral surface to the other. At this point, the bait cures in brine until thawed. Ernie employs a nifty trick for removing entrails: put the plug on its lateral surface and press the belly with your thumb while pinning the entrails to the cutting board with the dull side of the knife; then pull the plug and, *voila,* the entrails come away, leaving an absolutely perfect leading edge on the cutplug.

Careful rigging proves vital to the flip spiral he desires, as well as subterfuge. Pull the trailing hook from the inside to the outside of the high side (meat side) of the cutplug. Continue pulling until the leading hook eye pulls through the same hole. Take the leading hook across the back, inserting the hook in the short side of the cutplug and pulling the hook through. Twist the hook parallel with the spine and bury the hook eye inside the meat; the trailing hook eye is also buried on the long side of the plug, completing the deception. Ernie completes the rig and pulls his well-executed cutplug beside the dock. It flips — not spirals — once per second when drawn, then drops in a speechlessly tantalizing wounded motion so sexy you almost want to jump in after it. This represents the glide part of the power-mooching technique. Then it lifts and springs into action as though escaping from a predator, thus cueing the salmon when the engine is flipped into forward gear.

In the mystery of dawn growing from cedar-drenched shores, the fleet makes the 20-mile run to Spider Island by green-bleeping GPS, a trip all the more impressive as we are moving full speed through dense fog, and have been instructed to not lose contact with the boat in front. This is followed by the important words that if contact is lost, the boat pulls up and gets on the VHF for the lead boat to zero in with its radar. As our trip takes us through a maze of islands and reefs, stopping needs to be immediate to avoid collisions of the rock kind.

On the last corner, we pass so close to the kelp-strewn shore that we are presented with the image of a wolf on a shore of horizontal light, lifting its water-dripping face from spiny purple urchins the size of plates. Then it drops back into memory as though it has never been.

Here we are, stripping Apollo-space-mission floater gear in pore-sweating Oriental heat; I recall Lord Jim and pith helmets, sun trickling sweat down Hyde Park cotton shirts as our boats choreograph themselves for a counterclockwise run at The Wall. I find it humorous to observe that virtually all fishing locations in saltwater B.C. have a spot called The Wall and also one called The Gap.

Again some measure of pleasure I feel in watching other good fishermen at their craft. This is motor-mooching of high finesse, a kind of ballet set to tide and heartbeat of wave. Following one another in a circle, the boats line up. Lines and banana weights are dispatched a mere 12 to 15 pulls. Now begins the stop-and-go, slow-motion dreaminess of motor-mooching. One boat after the other, barely a boat length between us. We move only when the boat in front re-engages forward gear; when that boat puts the gear in neutral, we follow suit and glide. Move and glide. Move and glide. Twelve boats in a circle. The only sound in the golden fog is splishing of water from chrome manifolds. Lines move on the move to 45 degrees, then settle on the glide to 90. Beautiful symmetry of boats.

From the fog rises a sound I will always associate with Vietnam; soon the resort's helicopter sets nimbly on a log. Out step two guests and into a waiting boat. The tips of limber rods tingle and red-coated guides shift. Almost too fast to be seen, two pulls of line are jerked from the reel, then the rod is lifted from its rest. Then two more quick pulls. At the slightest strengthening, the hooks are set, rod handed to the angler and the battle ensues. An opening in the fleet materializes — all boats work together to help clients land fish — and the fish-on boat follows the chinook into clear ocean swell. Soon the chopper turns the world on its edge and swings up into fog.

Later, at the gutting tables, the chopper guests display their tyee. Many 30-pound chinook are being opened, as well as halibut from a spreader-bar expedition to Choke Pass and South Pointers. Those who haven't caught a halibut will not have experienced their breath, which is not pleasant, though their white clear flesh is attractive to the tongue. Wild-eye snapper and jagged-tooth ling cod line the dock.

This is the same dock to which the fish packer *Ocean Investor,* my neighbour Gord Coutts and I tied up on our April transit of the Inside Passage from Prince Rupert. In that weather, the wind came down so hard it opened holes in the water in the dark. But this afternoon, in the summer surrounding a halcyon day, is water so blue it must needs be true in its promise of peace and safety. In fact, it seems impossible such a storm could be possible.

I stand by, assessing my hands for cuts from line and needly teeth. Ernie comes along with electrician's tape. Wound around a cut, he explains, the tape prevents pain and deeper cuts. This is one of the best tips I've ever received and pass it along to you for the time your hands are in so much water and brine your skin comes away like cottage cheese. For the fly angler, consider also that electrician's tape is slippery so when your line finger on your rod hand — your index finger — becomes bumpy with water exposure, wind some tape around it and the line will slip smoothly, not jerk across wet skin, sending untrue messages about the bites on the end of your line. The following mornings I stand in the dawn, faithfully winding black around my fingers before heading out.

As I come to understand the motor-mooching technique in which bait moves in slow motion, I learn that 70 percent of bites are tiny tiny nibbles that only tingle the rod tip, unlike the smash and run of coho pulling the rod tip into the water. Instead, setting the hook hard results in losing fish. The rapid-fire two pulls of line effectively stops the bait in the water; in fact, in the mere act of opening its mouth the fish will suck the cutplug down its throat. Only after the two pulls are fired out — and they must be fast to push the bait to the fish — is the rod taken from the rod holder.

Rod-holding technique also must be sharpened. For those who hold the rod in their left hand — and this includes most people, also left-handed ones like me — you put your right hand on the holder to keep it from moving and with your left pull the rod from its tube. The rod comes up in a split second every time. Do it any other way and it takes many seconds, seconds in which the fish inevitably moves off, having discovered the hard, crunchy things in a tasty treat, things that have a different electrical potential than bait and thus lead to the bait being spat out. Note that once the rod is lifted from the holder, a second set of two pulls is fired from the reel. Whether the line stiffens or not, two sets of pulls are usually enough. There is a trade-off between pushing the bait into the fish without the weight of the sinker and firing so many sets of pulls that the sinker falls below the fish, pulling the bait away. Strike up after four pulls.

Blistering is the only word that describes the run of a 20-pound chum. One of my rods bends down so hard I can't lift its tip from the water. Over my shoulder on the other side of the boat, insinuated between my other two lines, a silver bullet cracks the air 100 feet away. Before I can do anything it runs another 75 feet and the image of it six feet in the air, sun glancing off a tail framed by sky, sears my mind. Beside me another boat glides by as I stand dumbfounded at the speed of my loss. Each brother raises a glass of chardonnay. "Boyo, you're supposed to look at the fish while you're trying to catch it," they tease and drift on. The bottle stands in its long stem, crushed-ice holder, a white napkin folded to keep the sun from bruising the fine liquid. Bizarre — urbane civility in remote wilderness.

That day I register 14 10- to 20-pound coho and chum so silver as to be almost identical. It is like looking into an ocean of coins.

The next day presents even more, in the surf line at Odlum Point. This is where the big chinook first enter Hakai Pass proper on their way around Calvert Island. Then they return up Fitz Hugh Sound before homing in on the Kilbella, Chuckwalla and Whonnock rivers. In an innovative move, the land- and water-based resorts fund a hatchery at Shotbolt Creek in Rivers Inlet, beefing up an already impressive run of 50- to 60-pound chinook.

The last morning, the fleet moves into the grey for The Gap and Barney Bay while I resolutely swirl the Odlum swell. Think of a day as a piece of paper upon which is written the will of another. Think of rain so heavy the rest of nature stops to listen and so the rain is largened. Add endless metal salmon and you have my final day. These are the fine hours, I think, bent like a saxophone player in the pounding rain under an impossible crooked moon. Monofilament wraps and cuts my hand, 20-pound coho lever free, the hooks become part of my shoulder, like some friendly, toothy, hungry alien. Beyond the lighthouse, Blenheim with its fringe of trees, rubber-faced sea lions drop from asphalt rock.

I quit at 12 salmon — to retain my karma; as I have mentioned, I am superstitious about flying and a 13th would be dangerous. A solid seam of wake pushes steadily from the stern. The scuppers are awash with green indifference. I accept the beauty of a pink ocean when sun is an octopus, stealing from the old men that cedar become. I am here and this is good, I think as the Grumman Goose chicanes Kwakshua Channel to meet the cloud.

As Far As You Can Go

On the edge. As far north as you can go. Riding the border. All phrases that describe the glacier palace of the Nisga'a First Nation — Wilp Syoon. The lodge lies in the lee between two islands, afternoon sun hot on the deck. Below us, the sweet fluidity that is Spey casting in the hands of a skilled practitioner. Mark's orange line extends through the sun.

As all Spey anglers know, Spey casting was developed for the shallow, broad rivers of Scotland, with greenheart wood-core rods brought from New Guinea and weighing as much as four pounds. It is hard these days, in the time of high modulous carbon fibre and Kevlar from the aviation industry, when a rod of 10 ounces is considered a cannon, to believe the fly person could cast such a heavy rod all day without beating the shoulder joint apart.

Spey casting was developed for moving water, not still, and Mark has to take that into account in trying to cast the line. There is, for example, no current swinging the line downstream to end on the "dangle," as they say, whence all traditional casts begin. These casts, the double Spey, the single Spey, and the more recent snake roll, snap T and circle C were developed to change the angle of the flyline 45 to 90 degrees, thus bringing it from below to level with the caster. All of these casts originated from the roll cast, which most use today to bring sunk tips from their watery handshake and then follow, on the surface, on the dangle with one of the casts already mentioned.

The small line of bubbles marks the line's rip from the water and is the time, as Simon Gawesworth says, of the white mouse. The supple double Spey first lands the fly close to angler and then the rod tip leads the line wide like a dancing skirt following the tip to a crisp stop at 1:00 and 1:00 PM. Then, the wait for the belly to form behind and the cast directly out on the water from the float.

In the morning, Mark rides the helm and the shushing water down the long Portland Canal. I am on the Canadian side of this 100-mile channel, he on the American. Gumboots up on the dash, we ride the slow sea to Indian Head. Mark is a nice-looking lad down the lens of my camera, his yellow rainslicker and cropped black beard.

Mark's version of motor-mooching takes some time to learn. An antithetical method that takes me days to figure out. The cutplug descends connected to a downrigger. When the tip tingles, I am instructed to break the rod from the clip, but instead of reeling slack and striking the hook, I am told to fire two pulls into it, and then two more, before sticking. A method to my mind that seems the opposite of the right way to do motor-mooching — with a six- or eight-ounce lead weight but no downrigger. Still, I am having a chinook pull me around the boat, up on one side, around the bow and back down the aerial side, holding on with my other hand. It has to be admitted that the method as practised has put a hefty fish on the end of my tether.

"Herring report for July 19." These words come from the VHF.

I am sliding around the back of the boat and wondering why. When I look down, the answer is clear: there is blood on the floor.

"You got your herring and you got your sardine and you got your pilchard."

And then I see the blood is coming from my right hand. This is always the way, I think. Fishing and my blood go together. A Murphy's law. One of the handles on the single-action reel has broken away from its screw and each time the reel revolves the screw slices my palm. More than a dozen circular cuts.

"Over at Indian Head, yeah? Over by that good Indian face. They're brailing right now."

We have been trolling right by this unusual rock formation, sticking out of the shoreline in bright white and green and yellow rock the shape of an Indian face. We have been getting nothing until now. We trolled down, we turned, we trolled back and in the time it took to turn, a seine net has been extended for a shore set by a tough aluminum work boat. The big chinook fin by, way down right against the rock.

"You see the net?" the VHF goes on.

"Where is this guy, anyway?" I've got my foot on the transom yarding up a silver-and-black chinook of 35 pounds.

"He's down past the big commercial boat."

"He's just gathering the net now. And you can see the squishers in the drum," the speaker intones. The stern drum rolls the net in and trapped fish are being caught against it. Each one is pressed so hard it rips to pieces.

Gathered, the net is lifted into the air. I hand Mark the rod and get down on my hands and knees. My mainline swings to me. I take the pliers down the line to the barbless hooks and turn them over. The fish looks up at me, I am conscious that it looks right at me and through me and then it heads over in a roll and sinks out of sight. Eerie.

"Ya see that river of blood?" The speaker is referring to the six-inch blood pipe dropping from the purse.

"Ah, yeah," Mark says into the speaker emphasizing the "yeah" and laughs. Immediately I am concerned. The way he has said it is an imitation of the Indian guides and owners.

In the seiner's net are a couple hundred salmon from where we have had only one bite. This tells me that even when you don't get a bite, there are hundreds of salmon down around your line. I line up a half-dozen, semi-frozen, seven-inch herring that have been getting toughened in brine all morning. Brine is tough on the hands, too. A week after I get home from a trip, all the skin on my hands peels off, making me look like a leper. Mark's hands look like ricotta cheese from their summer's exposure.

My usual practice is to slice off the heads with my left hand, reach over with my right, picking up the heads and tossing them over the transom into the swirling eddy of the engine. Instead, something I have never done before, and for no reason whatsoever, I slice the bait, pick up the heads and throw the knife from my left hand. Before it's an inch from my fingers I yell the expletive that means two people making love.

"Yeah, eh, they drop the bag on that eight-foot by eight-foot tray. Look at them salmon hit down. And watch the deckhand stomping through them in his rubber boots."

The knife arcs out and plops into the water where it sparkles and is lost to sight.

"What did you do that for?"

"No good reason, I can tell you."

Mark puts his hand out in the air, palm up. "Well, I know it's all good and that but we could use that knife."

I, the big white hunter, who is expected to make no mistakes, am ashamed. And the Herring Report goes on. "You see that big guy, picking up the salmon to go back? It's not a sockeye, see?"

"Ah, yeah," Mark says into the microphone in his hand. Heavy accent and a tone or two below on the "yeah." I get it now, everyone says it that way and it's a way of getting along, a way to humour.

The unwanted salmon, that is, of a species they are not allowed to kill, is thrown by the deckhand. It hits a wire line and falls back into the boat where another kicks it through a scupper into the ocean. The next salmon is pulled up by its gills, something that kills most fish. Luckily, it is thrown clear of the boat's rigging. On the other hand, it falls a good 20 feet down to the ocean where it smacks the water and floats belly up.

"And that's our DFO fer ya, the Herring Report is telling ya not many of those fish brailed out — not our steelhead, not our chinook, not our coho — survive." This is perfectly obvious, given the amount of blood in the water and blood and slime in the boat. The gargantuan, unshaven captain tells us to get the expletive lost.

"This is brailing?" I say. If this is brailing, then there's no purpose in doing it. "This is killing virtually every fish they let go."

"Ah, yeah," Mark says and I close my right hand. Its circular cuts sting with salt. The Work Channel tide rip is forming ahead. The ring of islands through which the ocean expresses power are long and lanky, like big people who once lay down to watch the stars and understand what they meant. Now, these centuries later, they're looking up, still still.

When we motor to Dundas Island, it is as though we have intruded upon a scene we have no right to experience. So much of this coast never gets seen. There are no McDonalds' wrappers, no pop tins, no cigarette butts. And I'm rubbing at my nose and my ears and swatting around. I am also feeling subdued and foolish for losing the knife.

The Herring Report keeps on coming. And by now it has dawned on me that it is not a DFO broadcast; it is one of the lodge's boats. To my query, Mark answers, "Oh, we do the Herring Report to keep the other lodges from using this channel. We like to use it and if we keep it tied up, they move to another."

"Ah, yeah," I answer, looking out at an anonymous Emily Carr headland of big silver tree trunks and writhing green moss bulging to the rocks and their horizontal lines of black and white and yellow. The trees lunged out centuries ago and never got all the way.

"There used to be a lodge back there. It had to close down. So many no-see-ums, it drove the clients crazy."

And he's right. There are many blood suckers out in the outback, the mosquitoes, the ticks, the lice, the horse and deer flies, the leeches, but the worst are the no-see-ums. One night I was casting in the dark on a river, the black shapes of bats flying right up to the rod, moving up, across and down, never once hitting. I got 25 bites and my hands swelled up so I couldn't do much for a week. And the itch? Almost unbearable.

We have been out in the sun now for days. The tops of our ears and the ends of our noses are red and raw. I pick up the microphone and press the button. I say, unintelligibly, "Hay, huhh, hmmnn nenmennsktka ttisielahi," and am hysterical with laughter. Mark takes it from me and mumbles as though he is answering, and we laugh back against the stays, the chairs, holding our stomachs. From the speaker, comes an "Ah, yeah," and we are truly and fully beyond hysterical — there's no other way to put it — for minutes.

When I finish holding my ribs in with my hands to keep them from breaking, I yell, "Fish!" and Mark jumps to the rod, yanks it free, fires two pulls, fires two more and sets the hooks, rod tip high in the air. As all salmon are — there is no mystery here, it is why we fish, after all — this one is intent on being difficult to catch. It migrates from the downrigger through the engine leg and toward the downrigger on the other side. In racing after it, Mark trips and hits the transom well. The rod knocks from his hands and takes a flying leap into the ocean. This is a Lamiglas rod and an Islander reel adding up to $1,100 worth of equipment, sinking through the green.

"I just want you to know," I say, "that you've made me feel a whole lot better. At least I wasn't dumb enough to lose a rod."

"Ah, yeah," he says, as the rod flees down, pulling its halos of light.

"Let me cheer you up," I say. "Three strings — pieces of string, like — go into the bar. The bartender comes along and kicks them out, saying, 'No strings in the bar.' One comes back and the bartender kicks him in the rear end. 'I told you, no strings in the bar.'

The second string comes back and the bartender says, 'Aren't you a string?' 'Ah, yeah,' comes the response. 'Well, then get the expletive outta the bar.' The last string ruffles his hair and says he'll go get some off-sales. When the bartender says, "Hey, aren't you a string?' He responds, 'No, I'm a frayed knot.'"

And so goes our poor humour for the rest of the day. I have the evidence in my slides: a 48-pound chinook and the demonic glee of Mark.

Boots against the dash and boat loping back from Canada's most northerly saltwater fishery, back from the ocean, back from the pinnacles where we took our trip limit of halibut in one hour, back from Zayas Island's outer edges for green-as-they-come coho, back from Dundas with its major wall for chinook, back from Portland Canal. We ride the quartering sea, one wave and then another, underneath and then behind, glass ones, rooms of broken windows in the onshore wind.

"Ah, yeah."

Coming Home to Langara

I remember now, Twin Otter lifting reluctantly, coughing in the morning, from Aliford Bay west of Sandspit Airport. I remember those many years ago when I went with the Oak Bay Group to Langara. My first trip. I remember quaffing Scotch to keep my perspective on sure death. In my mind the plane turned over into a dive for the ground, a border none of us could pass through.

I remember the eagles riding the smoky moon like minor tonsured deities in the eagle-branch trees of bent Sitka spruce, arms ripped by incessant wind. I remember coming home, my hands so full of scabbed-over pieces of pus that I could not close my fists.

I remember, it was my first trip away, and it was mystical, the mist in the hallways, the underlying hum of generator all night long. I remember allergies, from which I got better but never got well.

And now, a decade later, returning to where my travels begat a thousand articles, three books and catchsalmonbc.com, the site of my greatest interest: passing on to other anglers the knowledge I have been fortunate to learn in my fishing career in finer places than most are able to go and with anglers as good as or better than I, with their knowledge of decades passed on to me. Fortunate am I.

And now, in the present that is no memory, the Twin Otter, wavering like a gull in an onshore breeze, moves north into nothingness that is fog over muskeg, the eastern side of Graham Island, the trees small because big ones can't gain a foothold.

And now the descent, ocean coming into view below, calm as things that are not alive, pontoons 10 feet from safety. We skim the ocean and our watch hands turn round. There is land out there in the sea, there is an island where I began: Langara. And Langara has a cliff that the more my digital "watch hands" strip off numbers, the more I mentally tell the pilot to put the plane down. Put it down on the dead calm sea, don't drill the bottom of fog as time moves on too far.

Anyone who has flown in an Otter knows that the pilot and co-pilot sit right in front of the passengers. There is one middle seat, right behind them, flipped into the aisle once they have bent-headed it up the cabin and jumped into their seats. I am on that seat and what I see does not make me happy. The co-pilot is taking out a map, usually a useful thing, but on second look I see it is road map, for driving the gravel roads in a car. At which point I am mentally shouting, "Get this bird on the water."

Then the co-pilot says something to the pilot and the pilot passes across a pen from his pocket. The co-pilot writes something on his hand and passes his hand directly across for the pilot to see. As I am about three feet from the hand, I also see, and what I see doesn't quite sink in: "We missed our mark," until the pilot pushes in the gas and pulls hard up to the left and we scream — or perhaps only I scream — up and away into the fog.

After circling for what seems hours, we end up back in Sandspit for the night at the Sandspit Hotel. Oak Bay has bought us toothpaste and toothbrush, the room and dinner, though the bar, nuts, is a no-host one. Past the door to the pub, as we eat our first meal in a long day, a very old guy walks in one direction, then a few moments later he walks past in the other direction, fingers to his lips. A few seconds later he passes again and tries down the hall behind the door, but doesn't seem to be able to figure out how the doorknob works.

"Seems to be a problem out there," I say and go out to see what's happening. "Are you all right?"

"The door's not here," he says through his aviator-shaped glasses with a gold bar across the forehead. "The door's not here." There is nothing to do with incomprehension but take his room key and guide him with his dignity home.

Next morning, the ceiling is a few hundred feet and an older pilot, one with shades and shorts and sandals, dials that thing in the ceiling of the plane and up we go for the hop across Masset and Naden Harbour and down to the waiting *Marabell.* A former hydrographic boat retrimmed, she serves as a mother ship in Henslung Bay.

The rooms, as always on a boat, are fitted well, with a tiny sink, closet above the foot of the bed, cupboards below the captain's bed and a mattress that curves with the curve of the room, exactly six feet long. The head is down the hall. The joiner's cabinetry is beautiful, mahogany and teak all round, in the lounge, the galley.

On the heeling docks is the largest bull sea lion I have ever seen. The sound of it breathing is a huge animal with bronchitis on a megaphone. Rocco they call it and try to keep it off the floats. When a halibut carcass goes flying from the filleting table, Rocco returns and, without hands, of course, tries to wolf it down, something far wider than his own mouth. And there is the breathing and breathing.

I am paired, and surprised, with the old gent who lost his way the night before. Two dock attendants walk him across the whaler-style boat's bow to the seat at the stern. In his hand is an ancient rod that looks like it was made in the era of aluminum rods, and a casting reel, the black body and silver handles and levelwind reel like an original Penn in the days when Hemingway rowed his own sea.

He is introduced to me as Richard and he begins, as loud as if I were down the dock a ways, cotton batting in my ears. "I'm a Dick. I'm a Dick," he says. And I think, fine, you're a dick.

Captain Ahab and his antediluvian gear are installed at the engine, an outboard, and he whizzes us through Parry Passage and around the kelp bed to Cohoe Point. I have always, upon coming to what was a significant setting for significant happenings in my life, the desire to see if it is as remembered the many years. And I find that it is. The long, slanting shore from a blip of a point, and under my eyes, on the moving screen, bottom deepens from 50 feet to a little more than 100. And Cohoe, the first of sequential points: Andrews, McPherson and No Name. I remember the gorging black bass, the hundreds of them behind McPherson, and how every time the tide moved me in, I took three lines of bass. I let them go and redid each plug, vowing not to come so close again.

I slice a few cutplugs from semi-frozen herring, leaving in the innards, which, almost frozen, are hard to twirl out with a knife. And down to 19 pulls the two side rods. Dick will fish his one down the centre. He looks at my cutplugs and cuts his own. In one hand he steers the boat, the other holds his rod.

"You have a different way of doing things. I'm not saying it's wrong, but it's different than I've been taught." This is Dick. I am looking at him quizzically, I guess, and he says, "Your bait, your bait. You left the entrails in it."

"Ah, yeah," I say, having just returned from Wilp Syoon, intoning louder and lower on the second word. "I know it's all good fish-catching stuff to get them out and make the slice around the cavity perfect, but I look at it this way: if the fish are gutted and the boys find the bait heads in them we discarded off the transom, doesn't that mean that way out here in middle of nowhere, it doesn't matter whether we take out the guts?"

Dick pushes his glasses to his brow. "Okay, fine, if that's the way you want it, that's okay and that may be the way you want to do it. I'm not saying it's wrong, but I've never seen bait done that way."

It turns out that Dick — and here my rod tip takes a quick trip to the water line and I leap upon it like a tiger with sabres for teeth, almost making Dick jump out the back end of the boat — has been coming to Langara Island for 23 years, a very long time. He's 87, and this no doubt accounts for his poor balance. He says he won't be coming back. "And you're a writer, too, I mean."

And I think: that day will also rise for me, the day when I no longer have the physical skills I have taken for granted for scores of years. Over Cohoe, clouds are the towering white elevators of the prairies. Making canyons in the sky, sun peers down through these cliffs, these pillars of cloud, purple and bulging like muscles.

As I have grown older, the need to fight, the need for anger has dissipated. I think that what you learn is to accept yourself and accept others. And I turn away from anger these days. In the way luminous seashore grass bends from wind, I bend away. If I need to be angry, then I want not to be with that person. Dick goes on to tell me he has been married 62 years.

"That's quite an accomplishment," I say, and it's true; my own parents are more than 55 years along, and two of their three children's marriages, my own included, are ended. And I wonder, in that generation, when they came to the point where one person must be bent and crippled for the marriage to go on, how the defeated one came through. No one in my generation will do that now. Dick has many children, grandchildren and now great-grandchildren.

"That must be nice," I say. I do not tell him that my own children, in my absence, have lost me. That my greatest pain has come not in marrying someone against my ambitions, but that after staying home almost a decade to bring up my kids, after the same distance into divorce, after asking their interest more times than I could, I finally had to deal with myself instead. And here, what an adult comes to, is resolve: when my children come into my mind, I put them out. That pain is detrimental to me. But, combined with this is the intention that when they may come to me, I bring none of my pain, I bring only the simple cloth of happiness. This destination I have not yet reached.

The day wears on and I have had the satisfaction of almost a dozen times bringing a keen silver-and-black-mouthed chinook between 20 and 30 pounds to the boat and rolling the leader around my jacketed arm — don't do this with bare, cuttable skin — so I could reach down with my left hand, find the hooks quickly and let the fish go without being touched. And so, too, has Dick taken a fish or two, the drag, its clicker, protesting what should be its finest moment, challenged by a fish stout and short and still 30 pounds.

Our boat scatters waves to the *Marabell* and a seagull flies beside us. It flies at the same speed as the boat. It flies in the same direction as the boat. It flies as though a string has been tied to it from the boat. As I put my finger out, its wing shows me its white underside and it peels off into distance, as Dick turns to see nothing. Isolate I am in the sound of the engine. There is nothing I can say that will reach him. I turn back with the odd sense that is left when the one you talk to has no idea what you are talking about.

At the floats, I step on the curved part of the bow and fall to the dock. I am quickly up, embarrassed, saying I am fine. Two dock guys take Dick on either side and bring him to the float, and he takes the railing once his foot is put on the floating ramp. What I mean is that one of the dock guys gets down and lifts his foot and places it on the ramp. He pulls himself up in his bright orange-and-yellow floater bib and coat.

Off the gutting table where blood rains down all day, the carcasses are tossed. Rocco, with his prehensile whiskers, catches them out of the air and, with that heavy, boozy, squeagy throat, crunches and crunches. He can get his mouth round a tyee head.

I learn from Dick that he is not that happy with having great-grandchildren. I think of my own life, how things have changed since I was a teenager, for example when a few girls were sent away to have their babies and those were necessarily given up for adoption. That was the only option then. "I'd love for my daughters to have children. I tell them," I say breezily, "to go out and get pregnant and bring the child to me." I laugh at myself and the times and the sentimentality of it all.

Dick pulls his chin onto his chest. "Well, it is different, for us, we were not so pleased to see those girls, at 15. Fifteen, I'm saying, do you understand? That is not for us." And I think, you are religious. That would make a difference in our views.

In the afternoon I come upon him sitting outside the lounge in an area with a dodger canvas around to shield it from the wind. He is sitting heavily in a deck chair. He is pooped and hair is plastered to his forehead and the rings around his eyes hang like long eggs.

"Take my boots," he says and I must look as though I don't know what he means, for in frustration he adds, "Take my boots off. I can't do it."

I wonder if he is angry about showing his frailties or at his growing inabilities. I can no longer bring my right foot to my head. My eyes can no longer see the eye of size 8 fly hooks. I tie knots with my eyes closed because I cannot see them, and it is embarrassing with my extra, over-my-glasses specs to magnify the hook.

I take his rubber deckboots off and he leans forward. We struggle to remove his heavy survival jacket. I wonder how nurses manage this. And he stands so that I can pull his bib down his chest and down his waist and down his legs, whereupon he sits and I pull them off his feet. I pull his socks back up his glass-smooth, white, angry-veined ankles.

In the hot room I put his rubbers toe to toe and hang his bib. In pulling his jacket inside out I receive a whack on my hand. I am standing between the bulkheads when I am asked, "What's the matter with you?"

"Er, ah ..." I look around without comprehension and then see the stream of red drops down my pants, the pool of blood at my feet, the red trail following me from the gear room. My right thumb reveals its bone beneath the blood, and I leave a trail all the way to the captain's quarters where I am given a packet of gauze. When it is full of blood and I am dripping on the floor again, another packet is applied. When that is full of blood and I am dripping on the floor, another packet. And so on. After 10 packets, I say that it doesn't look like it's going to stop and how about I get a few stitches. Later, I am cleansing my wound with a dark, reddish-orange liquid pad for 15 minutes before the surgeon pulls his sickle-shaped needle through one side of the cut and out the other. I have not had anaesthetic. I do not know what cut me. My hand lifts when he pulls the thread.

Then the next day, I am slicing herring with one thumb wrapped white and three times its size and a surgeon's rubber glove over top of that. The salmon are accommodating — and I should tell you what kind of angler I am. I am an action angler. I will willingly take 10 small fish rather than one large fish any day. I am most in my element in the pandemonium of a quadruple header, winding the rods over and under one another and through the engine, etc. Among the many salmon of the day are the memorable ones. Ones that will take themselves as high in the air as their tails can power them from the ocean. Fourteen miles an hour is what it takes to launch a fish from the sea. That's its escape velocity. I wonder how fast a humpback whale, all 747 size of it, must go to breach so there is a playing field of space beneath it. How many tons? I don't know.

I have kept two fish exceeding 30 pounds for family and close friends and neighbours, along with some fillets of coho for me, blast-frozen and vacuum-packed, the primo product from the topmost island in Canada's Pacific, from the peak of the Queen Charlottes.

I have also extended my double-handed rod, and when the sea is being quiet, I perform the pleasing symmetry of a single Spey off the bow. Dick has been fighting his fish from his seat for these few days so I leave my rod lying on the floor in all its $1,500 of value. Accordingly, I am less than enthused when he takes to chasing a 33-pound fish that dives the water like the sand worms chase through the movie *Beetlejuice*.

I wouldn't be happy with him moving around this low-gunwaled, fibreglassed skiff at any time, less so when there is an expensive fishing rod that I cannot get to, standing, as I am, with the net at the stern. A goodly raft of kelp has joined the engine as an ocean clot.

"Net the fish," says Dick. Sure, I think, the chinook that is as girthy as I am and rests vertically in the water; its uppermost part, its head, is about three feet under the water.

"Just hold on."

"Net the fish."

The mainline is nicely wrapped around the kelp and has got under the propeller. There is just no way I can do the proper catch-the-fish thing, i.e., the fish is led head first into the net. The net is held, excess bag in the extending hand; when the fish is two-thirds into the net, the bag is dropped and the fish, if it moves at all, only drives itself deeper into it.

"Net the fucking fish!"

I hunker on my hands and knees at the stern, reach down into the cold ocean, into the deep green from which we draw our selves and that which we most love. I am up to my armpits, my glasses an inch from the salt water. I grasp the mainline beneath the kelp raft and, in pulling it up, run my other hand down to the fish. I take the fish by each side of its gills, one cover in each hand. At this point it shivers, and I can understand its feeling unhappy. Also I know the hooks could easily transfer themselves from it to my hands. All I can do is hold while it shakes me and the back of the boat, raising so much water that I disappear. My foot hooks the bait box where it is joined to the deck and I pull both of us up to the surface and over the gunwale and into the boat where the fish, into whose needle-pin mouth I can put both of my fists, lies on the deck and opens and opens on the too-thin fluid we humans call breath and life for ourselves.

"You know," Dick says later, as we lounge along the railing in the afternoon sun, "you're not like me. You don't know anything about me. You haven't paid for this trip. I have. I have never met anyone who hasn't paid. Do you see what I mean?"

In the bay below, my attention is drawn between the *Charlotte Princess* and the *Marabell*. It takes me some minutes to understand what is happening. Rocco seems to be twirling in the water as though chasing himself most beautifully and has only chosen to do it on the surface. Then I realize there is more than one body, more than one animal, flippers like scarves in a twirling wind. Like one of those kids' windmills or real ones, the soft flesh of their sails. They move around one another, once, twice, three times, like the classical song where the voices turn like the lace wheels of Tibet.

I see a brown appendage in the air. It is perhaps six inches long and perhaps two inches wide, and each time Rocco rolls, his fleshy breath is followed by this brown thing. Finally I understand it is his penis. And that their moving together is an exquisite species of sex on a planet of things most wonderful, strange and individual.

Looking down, Dick seems to see only that the two are turning, if, indeed, there are two in his eyes. "You didn't know this, I didn't tell you. I am different. I have entirely other interests than fishing. But not you, you are different if you see what I mean. I don't mean it harshly, but let me tell you."

Rocco and his ladyfriend are making love between huge vessels yawing on their lines and the sound of strain at the end of the pull. "Something you don't have. I play clarinet. I have for decades. I and some others, we get together every Sunday in my basement. And we have a quartet of strings and me and we play the music of centuries ago and we play the music of God. I have more than $10,000 dollars of sheet music."

And I don't think really anything at all. I feel neutral about what he is saying, though I agree it does make one think; he has more than what he displays on this island the ice age missed 10,000 years ago. It left pillars of conglomerate rocks rising like huge African termite mounds.

He has been married 62 years and he and his wife must have reached some accommodation, perhaps she backing down from he-who-must-prevail to be okay. I don't tell him the odd bit of commonality: I played clarinet myself. Played Dixie, played jazz, played symphony, played brass band, played whatever I was told to. I just lean over and watch the beauty of Rocco, who, I think, must not have long to live, and so one can only say bravo, love on. There is only flight — a helicopter — left for me.

What Has Always Been and Proving That It Is

Karma – the sum of a person's actions in one of his successive states of existence, viewed as deciding his fate for the next; destiny.

In the fall of 1953, Roderick Haig-Brown raised his first large chinook to a dry fly in his much-loved Campbell River, in the Lower Islands Pool that he had already made famous. His interest for much of his fishing career was in trying to do things that had not been done before. This included, some 26 years earlier, in 1927 when he was 19, inducing the first large hook-nosed coho to take a full-dressed Silver Wilkinson Atlantic salmon fly in a small northern Vancouver Island stream in the Nimpkish River area — the first salmon, to his knowledge, to have been taken with the art of fly fishing.

Of the chinook that later rose into history, Haig-Brown had this to say, in the essay "Diplomat's Fish," in his typically brief, lucid, elegiac prose: "... a great handsome, green-backed, bronze-sided fish rolled up. He was well over

20 pounds and his nose seemed to meet the fly so perfectly that I almost tightened; then I saw it [his dry fly], still floating, past his gill-covers, along the faint bronze of his side, past the anal fin, past the tail."

He was 45 years old. A half a century later, in 2002, I find myself having faced the ineluctable stream of time that, regardless of your intentions and wishes, continues its roll like a river to the sea. For myself, 45 years of fishing, from prairie streams to Rocky Mountains, to the westslopes in British Columbia, to a decade or two of cutting my teeth on saltwater salmon fishing in the still-famous Saanich Inlet; even prime ministers Diefenbaker and Pearson had plied its calm waters for what was, in the late 1950s and early 1960s, the best salmon fishery in Canada.

The years moved by of their own accord and I found myself returning to my roots, to freshwater rivers. By the turn of the century, I had come, in my fishing vocation, to a time when pleasures of earlier years — the largest fish, the most fish caught — had faded and new experiences took their place. This included a move to fresh- and saltwater fly fishing for salmon and to an interest in trying, like Haig-Brown, fisheries that had yet to be researched and properly developed.

That is not to say that I have been the first. People like Brigadier -General Noel Money, Jim Teeny, Trey Combs, Brian Chan, Kathy Ruddick and others have done much of the development of salt- and freshwater fishing from Clayoquot Sound to the Quality Lakes of the arid interior plateau of British Columbia. Nevertheless, having got to the point where I had moved on — in 2002, I landed more than 500 salmon, releasing 95 percent to carry on their way — I decided to stop keeping records of numbers of salmon, and move into recording in my daybook simply the specifics of technique, strategy and specifics of river hydrology that would inform the rest of my years.

West Coast Resorts which ran six lodges at that time (and still does) — in Tasu Sound, Englefield Bay, Whale Channel, Milbanke Sound, Eutsuk Lake and Rivers Inlet — asked me to come up to the Queen Charlotte Islands and help them develop their fly-fishing opportunities at Tasu Lodge. While bucktailing had at the time been proven, other aspects remained to make sure that a full package of fly fishing could be established.

I was intrigued by the chance to make this fishery into what it has become in the intervening years, and this is the story I wish to tell. The lodge on this large sound is the only one and thus "the lake of plenty" is a pristine area where low pressure will always be the norm — only the lodge's 10 boats fish a body of water some 15 miles long, with 3 inlets secluded within The Gap, as the dramatic western entrance is called, and more than half a dozen estuaries where spawners return for their rendezvous with sex and death.

Clayoquot Sound far to the south on Vancouver Island — and now known around the world — has four characteristics going for it: calm water; many square miles of shallow water, including the famous and classic structure, Catface Bar; loads of sandlance and herring; and sequential runs of migrating coho from May until late October when the local stocks ripen in the back bays before entering the many rivers to spawn.

Like Clayoquot, Tasu Sound has much to recommend it as a prime salt- and freshwater fly fishery for salmon: 25,000 coho, as well as pink, chum and sockeye that call the sound home; three very calm inlets; estuaries that allow for saltwater fishing in the shallow approach waters and, finally, in fresh water — in Tasu Creek just behind the lodge. Wearing waders one has as much as a mile of tidal river. Of shallow water, though, there is little; The Gap is 800 yards wide and perhaps 500 feet deep across its bottom. Other than at its entrance, known as The Hump, the only shallows occur in kelp beds where a boat can be tied to swinging stalks.

Terri Yamagishi, editor of the Japanese version of *Fly Fishing in Saltwaters,* and I arrive by chopper to a mizzly day, as they say in the Queen Charlottes. I notice wavelets by the lodge and know from experience that The Gap will be howling, with a 25-knot wind blowing right in the entrance. And it is as we lump and bump across the sound, with wind pushing the water in bins, wind funnelled by the mountains so it picks up twisters of water in its passage.

On each side rise steep, masculine mountains that show wave-raked black rock for the first 30 feet, a testament to winter conditions. Then a white layer of rock and a thin grazing of grasses and then trees, Sitka spruce smashed by hammers of wind and combed like wet short hair to the underlying structure of the rock-face bones.

The south side is as dramatic as any Hollywood director could desire, rising above the green and white-tipped waters with two huge rips that look as though a giant hand had taken the mountain and attempted to split it open like a loaf of black bread. After giving up, the hands left deep wedges for white splinters of water that fall from the clouds, wearing deep canyons in the rock face before falling into mist far above the wave-ravaged rock walls.

Having keel-smashed the boat through the venturi-heightened waves in The Gap, Ryan Peterson, our guide, begins untangling the lines of his personal and lovely motor-mooching rods, combining both black and gold anodyzed Islander reels and 10.5-foot Lamiglas rods. Smooth, silent, silky.

"But I'm a fly fisherman," Terri says and begins unfurling his fly rod, attaching a reel. Here we are in troughs and crests of six-foot waves, wind blowing foam into our teeth and the rain hitting our faces like pieces of wood. In other words, conditions are far too challenging for fly fishing. From the rods in their pipe stems, along The Wall as the south side of The Gap is known, 25-pound-test cutplug rigs stand to attention, horizontal to the water.

It takes 15 minutes of soft sell from Ryan to suggest that for this afternoon at least, conditions are unfavourable, and perhaps it's wiser to get some fish in the boat and try the fly the next day. Terri is resolute, adding, "I don't keep fish. I'm a fly fisherman."

Ryan rubs his goatee and it's my turn to suggest, pointing to the waves rising on the wall face, a different approach. First they slap the rock and surge up 8 to 10 feet and then, with a huge sucking sound, fall down the black, down the white and through a yard of gooseneck barnacles adapted to life at its harshest. First they flee up, then they are punched down, every wave, every day, every month and year.

The water boils into white and then aquamarine and then the dark green and Terri finally gives in — for this afternoon only. The herring is cut on that small bevel of 30 by 30 degrees, lateral to lateral and dorsal to ventral surfaces, the organs twirled out on a knife blade, and mounted on the leading and trailing 5/0 single Kirbed hooks in the simplest arrangement: trailer hook, pierced through the short or belly side, inserted at the silver-black lateral line, so that the point, facing the tail inserts, rotates until the shaft is buried, and then rotating the hook so that the eye points to the dorsal surface; the eye is then pulled beneath the skin, and the eye and shank pushed forward so that only the point shows perpendicular to the lateral surface; the leading hook simply inserts on the high or meat side up into the shoulder and the barb pierces the skin on the meat side, near the backbone. I give the cutplug and 8-ounce ball weight 30 pulls and as I'm setting it in the rod holder, Ryan yells fish. Instinctively, I yank the rod as high as I can and bury the butt in my waist.

The fish turns me to the stern and gives all that it can offer of its own Pacific strength. Now begins that union of purpose that combines angler giving chase around the boat and guide shifting gears, forward then back, and hitting the throttle to move the bulk of the heavy, one-ton, tough-as-anything-made-by-man, bullet-proof aluminum craft in a second to, as the saying goes, "Fight the fish close to the boat." Rain smears my sunglasses and wind tugs at my hood so hard the snap button pops loose, pulling my hat, sunglasses and glasses with it. My reel hand goes to save my glasses and the boat turns and turns again, scrolling across the white, wave-broken ocean. In the surge of tide and shattering of wave we are moved half a mile to the rocks on The Gap's far side.

After the long time that it takes to bring peace to the fish, it lies beside the boat on its side, such an archetypal image of fishing: the looking down, the ingot shining up. I admire the wild silver beneath my feet and tell Ryan to release it. With a guide's good sense for a meat client's purpose, he points out that perhaps catch-and-release should come after we have boated this fish. I agree and with his hands around the wrist and mine in the gills we "tail" the chinook into the boat — 28 pounds.

The afternoon carries on like this: set the rods and put the boat in gear to make the lines rise and then out of gear to let them straighten down, the boat jumping sideways in the slapping waves, so close to the rock there is less distance from the cliff than another rod length. And the tingling strike of a bait mouthed and two pulls of mainline snapped into the water, wait, reel with tip down and then strike up high to set into what the ocean in its rude benevolence gives forth.

The second is 26 pounds, which I release, and the third, on Terri's rod, pulls us in circles once more across The Gap and in to the rocks on the northern shore. First he gains ground, then loses the same amount again, and even more; the fish, with its head down, is difficult to raise. Its size is told by Terri switching the rod from one hand to the other to give the first a shake and rest. An hour after line snaked away, the chinook lifts its head clear of the waves and perfectly, body vertical, shakes its mouth back and forth while giving us the evil eye.

"Twenty-four pounds," Ryan suggests and I agree; the head gives evidence of a body of equal size. But the fish will not come and dispells our conclusions, having moved from the stern to some fair distance from the gunwale where it cleaves the surface from below, shouldering it aside like a football linebacker, its broad back parting the wave looming above us.

"That's no 24-pounder," I say and both Ryan and I begin the mental calculation. "But his head was so much smaller."

"Like a Columbian," Ryan offers, and he has a point; those early salmon are stubby in length but broad of girth. "More like 35." When the easy-slider and insignificant weight lift above the waves for the final time, Terri backs up across the boat and leads the fish head first into Ryan's net. It is not an easy passage, for the fish is so long that its tail will not fit inside.

The great fish requires both Ryan and me to lift the netting to bring the silver beating of life within the boat. Again the looking down, legs shifting on the shifting deck, green burying our rubber toes. The stern rises and then drops as the engine moves and is fouled by kelp. The engine whistle begins a shrill journey across the minutes and chests heave, we back into deeper water grinding the kelp to chunks. The fish is dispatched, perhaps the saddest time of fishing, for those who have fished long and found some kinship with the fish of their quest; for those who have killed so many they finally say, "I do not have to do this anymore. Let this fish move on, with the only life it will ever have." And I say in my head as I do with every fish that I catch, "Thank you." First to the fish and then, "Thank you for this day," spreading hands and addressing the wave-scabbed shoreline, the strings of whipped foam, the wild and hurried trees.

Measured, the fish is 43 inches from nose tip to tail fork by 28.5 inches in girth behind the shoulders and in front of the dorsal fin. It is a fine fish, one of deep chest, one who fought a great battle and must be admired for its tenacity. This is what the long-time angler comes to: appreciation of the fish for giving of itself, of having the good fortune to bring it close, and when the decision has been made to keep it, the bitter and the sweet of subduing it. Later, when lifted to the scale, the large chinook, having lost some weight through the day, still registers as 42 pounds and a large lapful of adversary on Terri's thighs. This is a fish that would easily, held by the gills, rise from the float to his chest.

My rod is placed in the rod holder and almost before its bait is lowered into the most remote of the remote fish-filled waters, Ryan yells me to focus. One of my wet hands pulls on the rod, the other braces on the rod holder, and as I turn the rod up in my left hand, a green-faced wave passes under the boat, pulling me from the rod. For the first time in my entire fishing life, a rod is separated from the tips of my fingers.

The reel buries itself in the face of the wave. Then I lunge over and down, my thigh smacking itself so hard on the railing the bruise, later, rivals a grapefruit in size. My shoulders and arms reach down over the side so deep that my face touches the crawling water. The tips of my fingers at the end of my arms touch only briefly before the rod is again lost.

Over my shoulder, the nimble rod owner Ryan, having registered the disaster, flies. On its way out of the boat, his left boot, in serendipity, is caught in my right hand. He is vertical in the ocean, inserted head first and all the way down to his waist, held only by the foot. The next instant I am pulling him back and he rises, soaking, rod tip in hand. An equal miracle for the grotesquely miraculous mistake.

Shaking with relief Ryan, in his adrenaline shudder, says, "God, *The Perfect Storm*, did you see that?" We are drifting sideways along The Wall, in the section where the cliff reaches out over the water and you are actually underneath the mountain as the waves twist and sheer the face of thousands of barnacles that are one moment mouth to the sky and the next mouth to the bottom.

Then the miracle turns, as instantly, to disaster. In his dive out of the boat, Ryan has smashed his leg across the ignition, the VHF, the gear shift and the throttle. The key is broken off in the lock, the radio cord has been stripped and the throttle assembly is split in two. I look up at the cliff over our boat and the short armlength we are from the rock.

For us, once more, good fortune shines this day. To the west of us, by sheer luck, another guide, Damien, has seen Ryan dive headfirst from the boat before the house-sized chop swallowed both him and me and Terri, along with the boat and all but the tip of the aerial. A line is hurled through the thick air and secured to the transom cleat. Then the snap of line, boat jerk and slap of wave up and over us and down into the boat. Ryan, now streaming water, clamps a long red licorice Twizzler between his teeth.

Later, towed home, and fed, sitting on the side of his bed, hands on his thighs, Terri offers in diffident, discreet, typically Japanese fatalism, hand over his mouth as though his words are too loud, sitting in his Polo pajamas, "I could see how badly you felt about that rod, as would have I." It is consolation, agreement, absolution. Then our eyelids close on the first day and it is no more.

The second day opens with a soft invasion of mist on the ocean. Below the float, like a type of cattle moving restlessly to pasture, a shape-shifting herd of white animals takes form beneath the water: perch like piranha where, yesterday, they pushed and shoved the entrails of the day's granting of fish. Ribbons of milt sacks, bludgeonings of flesh and, always, blood seeping from the filleting tables. The knives are so sharp I fancy I can hear the swish they make transiting the air, feel the slipperiness they make in your palm and then the surprise of blood.

The previous night we studied each other's flies: the true polar-bear-hair bucktails, beautiful in their long streamer length; my surface-film bucktails with a tiny spinner and narrower silhouette; lodge manager Michael Coyne's Clousers and the Purple Skunk, perfect for tea-stained northern streams running through boggy ground saturated with centuries of cedar; and my three boxes of various types of estuary and freshwater streamers, glow-in-the-dark, bright metallic colours for coho and the rest.

Tasu Creek winds its shallow miles out of the forest and in August receives pink and chum and, early in September, coho salmon. It is our job to see whether they will take the fly and whether we indeed have a pattern that will induce them to seek it out with regularity. The boat's wake crisscrosses the silent dawn and Michael explains that to fully scope the inlet's potential we need to sleuth the various creeks, of which there are a half dozen that support salmon.

When we arrive I find to my dismay that the tide is fully at its outward reach, leaving the whole estuary of green tufts of grass and orange of bladderwrack exposed. I say dismay because my experience with estuary fishing is that the bite is at its lowest when the ocean is as well. A less propitious tide could not be found. In my gumboots I wade the first riffle, noting that when the tide returns, this will be the first obstacle where the salmon will pause, waiting for it to be filled.

Prudently observing the large black bear on the beach — we are later informed that these are the biggest black bears in the world — Terri opts to cast from the boat, while I wade the outbound gravel that curves up from the sea so like a moon in its birth that I name the bar New Moon. Its structure leaves a shallow run that, because of the black algae common in peaty stream bottoms, easily secretes any fish hovering there in their stations.

This shallow run forms across from a basalt rock I name Volcano, sure that in ocean's fall the seam at its downstream edge will hold the salmon in place. Once the water has begun its rise, the seam on its upper edge will swirl the fish across what is now a wide flat meadow of barnacles and plum-sized rock that Dolly Varden and sea-run cutts should favour. Of the two indigenous trout, it is the sea-run, in its lovely, brown-dappled, silver-sided sea version, that cannot help leaping to show off its fine breast buttons.

I pause in mist that lifts wearily from trees and watch Terri for the love of symmetry. This is one of the pleasures of fly angling: his touch is sure and soft and aggressive and, as the cast lengthens, unhurried, easily hauling line and shooting it with a precise and fluid tug return, tug return. The many years he spent chasing the spooky bonefish and trout of his Colorado home have left a lovely, beyond-80-foot cast that straightens nicely, turns the fly over and settles softly on the water.

At this point, my own experience is limited. I have only fly-fished for 4 of my 45 fishing years and all of these for less cautious fish. I am a west-coast salmon fisher and with a sunk swung-fly presentation, it hardly matters whether the fly fails to turn over completely or is drilled a foot under water from failure of trajectory. Provided the fly and line land some distance above the fish — in roiling water — mending takes care of the mixing currents; it will either swing the fly on a bellied line across the face of the belly-to-bottom salmon, extend on a connected line as it swings across the lie or finally, in typical "greased line" fashion, particularly for chum — a strong upstream mend — pass the fly butt directly downstream into the noses of the resting fish.

From much practise at home in Victoria, my average cast, at this stage of my fly-fishing lifetime, will unfold 70 feet so that I may cover a fair bit of water and wade to where I have greater advantage. This past season I have worked on coiling line over my successive fingers — a technique Atlantic salmon anglers will know: from pinky to index, take 10 strips on the pinky, 8 on the next, 6 on the next and so on. The purpose of this is to keep the loops from tangling and to shoot the greatest amount of line when its backward journey would hit a tree or grass. The alternative, stripping into the water, leaves the rod to try and rip the line from the clutch of water, rather than, once loaded, simply pulling the line from the fingers.

Now, a typical sparse beach streamer, size 6 or 8, on a silver hook — a bit of pink thread, short silver body and two layers of pink buck-tail — is cast across to Volcano and allowed to sink and straighten before the strip. And shortly, with the first fish beginning to swirl after the passing wake, I am rewarded with an aggressive bite upon the tiny tuft of pink. When brought close it is a buck pink salmon in prime ocean condition, eight pounds, fly in the scissors of its mouth.

Satisfied with this, I start changing flies. Below me on the New Moon extremity, Michael connects with another pink, with his favourite fly, one that will stimulate the fish in this stream, so dark its four feet cannot be penetrated by the eye. A short purple-over-white Clouser is his fly of choice: the contrasting white is the key.

The tide begins its pendulum rise and Michael and Terri are in the boat. I am wading, watching the fish move up in small schools of 8 or 10. Above First Ripple a short run extends up to an abrupt 90-degree corner. I name it Big Bend. It has a lovely little pool formed by the river flowing over gravel and into the deeper channel, where a solid rock face turns the water and scours the hole. Its boulders in another stream would be steelhead-holding water. I am on the outside of the curve and must wait for the tide to rise and the boat nose to retrieve me.

The tide has risen to Big Bend by now and the opposite shore is an open meadow of green tufts. This straight-line run has a crease three feet deep where fish slither up from Big Bend. I name it Panama Flats and, looking upstream, note that it runs from under a large tree before crossing the small "valley."

Terri begins taking down his rod, saying, "Oh, you know, a travel writer gets spoiled." Here we reach a soft disagreement; our longings for connection with fish are not to the same degree. I am by nature an action person, and patient. I will take hours to deduce the swing of the fly toward the fish until I have with regularity begun to take the inhabitants.

I place my packsack on the ground and a black spot appears above me that after some moments begins to move. It is the bear, come back to the shallow above the next pool, perhaps to try for salmon. I feel he will have difficulty, the water being of a depth that favours the ocean-bright and full-of-vigour fish. In real life, bears are clumsier than depicted in documentaries. If the river is deeper than the legs that must then swim, few salmon will end up between the teeth in the black snout.

I have tried a standard Mickey Finn and a bushy pink blob of a fly that looks pretty goofy to me. My preference for freshwater is the lower silhouette and the simpler fly, for it rides lower in the water and perhaps hooks, at penetration, more securely.

Then much slow and noisy sidling up to the next bend. The pool's porpoising fish have me much enthused, because this behaviour, as opposed to jumping clear of the water, spells turned-on fish ready to chase down interlopers. Having not brought a Muddler Minnow — as I believed our time would be spent only on salt water — I am rueful. This well-known spun-deer-hair fly is vastly underrated in freshwater for salmon. It is a loyal little fly, drab, but clearly visible in both dark and bright waters. And a little something else, too. As the reader will know, it represents a minnow, complete with a red tag at the tail and red under the collar to imitate the flare of gills of escaping fry.

My feeling, having captured more salmon on a Muddler than on all other flies combined, save a yarn fly (which most would agree is not a fly at all), is that Muddlers stimulate an aggression-based response. That is, the salmon thinks it sees a fry and its response, swilled with hormones is: this is my spot, you go find your own. Alternatively, but this seems less likely, perhaps the smaller "fish" is seen to represent egg-robbing trout that need to be moved from the redd.

My fly sinks and passes below me on this little bank above the run which, on a sunny day, would be a poor spot to stand as your silhouette or shadow would be clearly visible and spook the salmon in their lies. Then my fly connects with a much larger fish than the pink salmon we have caught below. It is a sure connection and the fish moves rapidly down current, my flyline giving chase in an arc across the pebbled water into the softness above the seam in Big Bend below. All of my flyline has fled the reel. The backing is disappearing too. Time to give chase, or more accurately, waddle in gumboots and rubber waders and bib, and a thick, neoprene survival jacket. Far below, the first leap reveals the faint bars of a chum, one perhaps of 13 pounds, and then a lateral line of black, a clear indication of a doe.

Chum is the species I prize most among the salmonids because they combine the qualities of coho and chinook; that is, they leap and zing line at crazy angles like coho but have the power of chinook to turn and go, leaving me clinging to the rod and racing down the bank in pursuit. But when this fish is lying on its side, I find it foul hooked. Chum are not as good as the other salmon in hitting the fly with their mouths; most facial hooks can be taken as proof of a slash at a fly and a miss — but not this fish, hooked, as it is, in the side. So it cannot be counted as proof of anything more than that the chum are here early, on August 26, in this northern stream. In my home waters it will be October before the runs arrive, on the waves of the first monsoons that drench and close the summer eye of the coast.

I lever my leg over the gunwale and the boat moves upstream with the tide, the 70-hp Johnson trimmed as far up as we dare, to keep the water intakes in the water but prevent the prop from being twisted into Swiss cheese by contact with rocks. Here the stream has a fortunate pool that combines water five to eight feet deep with the stream channels rejoining one another on the tail of a grassy island.

Furthermore, a small creek, barely wide enough to require a leap, enters. And thus is formed a good holding spot: trees on the far bank for cover, a shallow and forbidding glide above and also freshwater for the fish to stop and scent, particularly the coho, which spawn in trickles of water so narrow it seems impossible the race could be continued under such harrowing conditions of birth.

The boat is anchored and the fish are put down. But 10 minutes later they begin to rise freely, porpoising, in which the head touches and reaches above water and then the turn, shoulders showing, the dorsal fin, the camouflage-coloured flank, the peduncle, the drunken-spotted tail and, at the last, the bubbles released from the mouth. Soon we are rewarded with several fine pink salmon, all seemingly clones of one another, at eight pounds each and all bucks.

"Do you know whether the bucks, which are generally the most aggressive, precede the females into the river?"

"Good question," Michael answers, "We'll have to see what we catch."

These are sure, willing stops. I swing the Clousers through their curve, but not a single bite is received prior to stripping; this means the fish are actively seeking the fly and taking it, rather than the swinging fly foul hooking or flossing. For the uninitiated, flossing refers to the leader passing through the mouth, thus pulling the fly into the outside of the far side of the mouth, or operculum. Flossing can be prevented by taking two steps upstream and casting again so the fly comes cleanly in front of the fish and is taken surely and intentionally.

At this point Terri, who has been on the bow platform, comes to offer me one of his reels. "When we bucktail, you may find that your floating line will not sink enough to bring the fly under water." And so, in unspoken agreement, we lift our lines to smooth over his impatience for moving on. Up comes the anchor and the boat drifts downstream through silence of mist and the piquant, acid colours of northern fall.

We pass the lodge on our left and its small island of trees, so small, so accidental it looks among this land of mountains and streams and never-ending rain, an improbable oasis in wilderness. We cross the long reach to Botany Bay, past Shearer Rocks. By Lomgon Creek the incoming tide and 25-knot breeze are in our face and rain streams across our cheeks. On the left, Eagle's Nest marks the inner and calm side of The Gap. The split black mountain prevents wind from curling round the corner, but the incoming seam deposits coho that stage and ripen for weeks before committing themselves to the streams within the sound.

Bucktailing speed is 1200 to 2500 rpm. Michael and Terri opt for an intermediate sink, and beautiful, seven-inch, polar-bear-hair bucktails for their sinuous, pulsating qualities that bucktail fibres do not possess. So beautiful a fly are they it is a shame to put them in the water. Nevertheless, two flylines fully extend, including 30 yards of bright orange 20-pound backing. But not mine.

Before I have rigged my surface-film bucktail, the ones developed in Clayoquot Sound, Terri's rod has its tip become one with the ocean, which is to say the rod almost pulls clear of his two mitts. The coho does what it wants to do, which is first appear in the air in front of the boat and then, with singing line slicing the water, appear at eye level behind the boat. It has Terri chase around the boat while I keep nets and rods out of his way.

After the coho "roll" — presumably a defense mechanism that looks like a diamond gone berserk — the fish grudgingly calms beside the boat. When tailed for lifting, it does as all coho do, makes one last run for freedom, giving the tailer, in this case Michael, a good face wash. He lifts it for a photograph, water streaming through his beard.

When the lines have been let out, my bucktail looks pretty silly 15 feet behind the stern, improbably skipping from crest to crest. To the dubious looks of my partners I say, "Well, it's true this is not intended for such high speeds." But my faith is rewarded. Soon my flyline lifts from the surface, connected to a fish, and then disappears along with the rest of my flyline before I can turn the reel over and apply more drag. I look at the guys and make the self-satisfied smile of the Michelin Tire Man, playing well into the backing.

It is a see-saw afternoon, half of the time spent across the wind-driven line of water beyond the Eagle's Nest back eddy, in the open wind and water spouts of The Gap. At one point, back to the wind, I feel the boat lift up so that from the stern, I am looking way down at the bow. Each time we pass from calm to storm, our fly-lines fly like flags beside the boat. A willing coho surprises us along what on a calm day would be a fine seam. As all salmon fishermen know, seams represent two streams of water, one moving, one not, or at least moving slower or in another direction. This concentrates the non-motile plankton and the baitfish that feed on them and thus the salmon, too. Fast-moving bucktails are more suitable for taking surface salmon, i.e., coho, than the deeper-running chinook. The latter we will attempt to capture with lead-heavy sink tips and deep-line techniques.

"The excitement makes them bite." Michael's long-soaked hand looks rippled as low-tide sand.

"Just have to have that thing," I say, skipping my spinner in the wash.

Many fine coho from 8 to 13 pounds accept our offerings. And to my pleasure, the surface-film bucktail invented and refined by Shawn Bennett in the Clayoquot Sound fishery takes four coho right behind the boat.

"Well," Michael says, "not as large as the ones we caught. Something to do with the size of the fly." I laugh. There is nothing to defend; I landed more fish than either of them.

And later, after dinner and too much wine, we retire for the day, Terri in his blue-and-green plaid pajamas with a small red polo player off-centred on his chest. From his side of the darkened room he says, "I have fished a long time and I make the whole experience one of my own. I do not need so many fish or ones that are such a struggle. Yesterday, I felt I must catch that fine chinook to please Ryan. I myself had already gone past the point of pleasure and felt I was in jail with that fish."

His offhand, self-deprecating, small laugh coming out of the dark needs no response, yet I feel I should be gracious. "It was a very long time, a fine fight, but yes, long, and Ryan is young." A kind of agreement.

"I do not wish to hurt the fish and do not wish to keep them. You remember that I photograph only live fish before their release. In this way my karma is maintained."

"Oh," I say casually, in confirmation, in humour, "superstition." I do not intend insult. I always say that fish talent is all in the hat, so you can't wear an ugly one. I also know there are, indeed, lucky anglers and they are better in your boat, though they rub your nose in their unbelievable luck.

But my words are met with silence on the other side of the room and I see my poor choice has suggested criticism. The thrum of the generator comes through Queen Charlotte dark and the points of rain swim before the window like the ends of a girl's long hair. Just before sleep, I say, "Yes," and in those last moments, I realize that my own deliberate thanking of fish and then nature, my mindless ritual, in its way may also ensure there are more fish to grace the end of my line and lift the charge of emotion from my belly. Superstition. Karma. We have come to the same place and I must tell him so.

On the third day when we rise, I begin the long issue of packing pack and camera and checking off items a sport-fishing journalist must take to the field, including flash, wide-angle, macro, batteries, film, etc., all double-wrapped in Ziplock freezer bags. Along comes an assortment of flylines, a few boxes of bucktails, saltwater flies, salt beach flies in their shorter length and, finally, river flies, the shortest of all and made with soft bronze hooks so any unremoved will soon rust and fall away from a fish's mouth.

Behind the float a restless bear crosswalks on the orange shore, the black and barnacled rocks. It stops at the thick rope and seems to consider. Surely it can smell the feast of good food items coming with the breeze in the white room of drizzle. It touches the line with its paw as though intending to tightrope-walk across to the lodge.

I mention this to Ryan as he turns the engine over. It chugs up over the moisture and early morning. "One of them, and in fact there are three that come regularly, actually swam out and had to be persuaded to plop off the float. So it's not unlikely our friend over there would use the line to its advantage."

Rooting in my pack I realize that the reel Terri has lent me is not there. I check the boat we were in the previous day and run through all my stuff three times, including zipping across the float to my room and going through the contents of my bags. Finally I have to concede the reel isn't among my stuff and, as it was in my bag, it is my responsibility. Glumly, I tell Terri the news and he is supremely disappointed.

"That was a special reel to me. I caught my first marlin on it and a 50-pound dorado. It's not so much the cost of the reel and line, but that it has so many fine memories attached to it."

I calculate that the reel, before line and backing, is $650 US and represents a significant sum to me. How such bad fortune is possible I do not understand. Only my second disaster on this one trip — the first averted solely by the nimble velocity of Ryan Peterson. And then I scrutinize the capricious, the vexatious Queen Charlotte air.

Michael Coyne has left me his rod and its intermediate line — should I even be touching someone else's gear? — along with its bright, fluorescent, Day-Glo-orange backing, all 500 yards of it. Soon we are in the lee of the Eagle's Nest with the wind coming in sheets of white around the corner, pushing the flood tide. A most welcome sight.

Each time into the blast, our thin orange lines crisscross the nervous stern. Water lifts in spirals, in funnels, spun in the constricting Gap. They come striding in from the sea, weird, *Lord of the Rings* trees with knees bending as they pass of their own accord the little Earth, the mustard-stained shores. We turn with Ryan at the console eating Twizzlers once again, wiping his goggle eyes with a finger. In the water, the beauty of the fluid, sensuous polar bear hair, in its softened white, its blues and greens, over spots of red and silver — a herring shooting at rocket speed through the water.

My guess is that the bucktail does not — and these are easily several inches longer — represent a true baitfish, but rather the shape of flesh as it tracks around corners. The fly stimulates the coho to turn and speed up to match the bucktail and then excites the fish into nabbing as best it can. Coho are the most curious, the most excitable of the five species. On a clear day, when you can stand high and watch green coho this far from our usual, humdrum, daily reality, you will see that the plop of a fly causes them to turn and streak in. The speed or glitter makes them nip, even if it does not look like any specific baitfish. After all, spinners cast by gear fishermen in freshwater can draw coho from as much as 25 feet, and this is when the feeding instinct is completely gone. They cruise after the piece of metal until they can't help themselves but grab with their only appendages — pin-prick teeth that regularly scrape my hands from wrist to fingertips.

Terri's wonderful, full, bushy creation receives the first strike, a most unusual one. First the rod tip dips as though something elastic has impeded its travel, then it is released and in the split second when the fly fisherman wonders what has happened, the release is replaced by a pure stoppage of the line so memorable — the stop of a steelhead in a river, for example — one knows by instinct it is a fish and not rock, weed or impediment. And then the fish hangs in the clear air above the pushed water and the boat wallows in the troughs.

Ryan turns the boat toward the fish and Terri does that kind of prayer common to fly anglers with reels of limited size. The fish flies toward the boat and the reel, one with a smaller-diameter arbour than the single-action trolling reels onboard. Raising his hands over his head, Terri moves backwards, while Ryan turns the other way, the boat crossing the galloping waves with aggression and intention.

The coho appears in front of the boat and Terri holds his rod high in the bow. In over-size bib and boots and yellow plastic coat, he stumbles the aisle littered with net and thermos and harpoon rinsed with living sea. Past the unscrewed seats. Past the flung-open tackle. Past the bleeping console with its waving spaghetti aerial, the prop and its churning brew. The last few feet are the death spiral we have come to know. Something crazy spins the green, sends flashing-neon-speed the eye can scarcely follow. And finally it is at boat side, apparently coming to hand. Ryan leans far over, taking no chances with 15-pound test, and takes it by the waist. This sends it into frenzy until, finally, it has no slack-jawed choice about a quick photo op and then the gentle bathing of water, the closing of its mouth, the opening of its gills. A quick snap of a square tail and the fish becomes nothing but salt water down Ryan's face. His hands look ancient, as ours do, too, skin that has spent too much time in water, and the blue-white ridges that it brings.

The lodge at Tasu Sound added, in 2002, a very good feature in the lee of Mount Moody — with cloud curling from its forehead, it is indeed a moody place, a place far removed from humanity. A small float and tent have been anchored so anglers can come in for a hot meal, close to the fishing ground, and not have to return to the lodge and then bang back into the wind to The Gap.

We have been most fortunate in landing and releasing 9 coho from 6 to 13 pounds, especially when we learn that another boat bucktailing has landed only one. Deciding what to do, we inscribe circles of white on the slosh of wave.

Over our radio comes word that the wind off the Pacific side of Tasu, off The Wall, is peaking at 50 knots. We decide to explore another world. In Botany Bay, the long flat blackness is calmer than a dream and we push into the mist, as though the only human beings to ever explore the island-studded water and the steep, tree-softened slopes. We are Martin Sheen up his version of the Congo River, ever and unerring to the shaven Marlon Brando pate and the patting of his fingers. Any moment, we might breast a dugout canoe come across a thin skin of centuries. We are hushed in a gentle curve of horsepower moving up to meet the estuary.

As with the other creeks, the grass-verge green and orange are so harsh they leap into the eye. The yellow of first fall, the tongues of tea-coloured waters and the green so green it doesn't look real, the black that is the ubiquitous bear. It is said the Queen Charlottes have more black bears than anywhere else in the world. This one moves across its landscape, nose to the ground. Then we see the soft swirl on the liquid black. I am let off upon the bladderwrack. The bear moves out of sight but not out of mind. As the boat drifts in the shallows, Ryan begins with the paddle to move after the fish for Terri, standing on the bow and reaching out with his long white line.

I am stalking chum in brackish water. I am stalking in oversized gumboots, water within a smidge of their tops. I hold my breath and cast, freeze to avoid disturbing the fish. But we are without luck. Our flies have not included estuary offerings — for example, a White Woolly Bugger, or a garish leech of chartreuse or bright orange over black, colours the keta-teeth bucks prefer.

So, we do not solve the riddle of this estuary so far from humanity it has yet, in our third millennium, to be named. This place inspires the mind to relent its boundaries and open, so nature in all its insouciance can win the heart. And fill your boots, too; the tide has turned and I am now on an island, and in getting back to the trimmed boat, I am soaked to the top of my thighs. I wave away concern and push my arm in a grand sweeping movement, one that passes Lomgon, passes the lodge and ends in the freshwater behind.

We return down the inlet that is as calm and secretive as the heads of Easter Island. We skim the silent, unyielding face, a double us reflected on its cool mirror. I am told, as speed rips away our words, "If you don't go and get dry clothes on, Terri and I are going to throw you off the dock so you have to. We don't need to play with hypothermia." Soon the boat nudges the others linked by bow lines to the float.

While changing clothes, putting on dry underwear, pants, socks, boots and new rain slicker bib, I realize I have been given good advice and that my wish to wail on the fish of Tasu Creek without stopping in was getting in the way of good sense.

Terri and I are let off at Volcano to walk the orange beach with its tufts of day-old green beard showing through. Up and down like structured birds we pass, but it is obvious that the reel, if it were here, has been lifted by the passing tide and carried away. The tide follows us up Panama Flats, to The Junction, where the stream channels reunite behind Bear Island and the seasonal No Name Creek flows out of the wilderness like blood from a heart. Above the pool is Flossie, a shallow where flossing is an obvious "technique." Above that is a classic glide I call Goldie Glide because upstream, three too-inquisitive bears lounge around a log jam. And so it becomes Bear Jam.

The fish — pink, coho and chum — scatter like below-consciousness dreams, dark lines in dark water and the algae black on black stones. Terri gives up his casting and puts a tentative toe on the tougher-than-terracotta bow. His hand is taken and his diminutive frame hoicked upon the deck. After some time watching his fluid thing-of-beauty stroke and the 90-plus-foot line land with a dry-fly guy's above-the-water-trajectory, I ask whether he minds my coming from teetering on the transom with one foot on its three-inch wall and the other on a one-foot hatch cover.

Terri is older than I, and perhaps his attitude will be my own some day. "I am enjoying the exotic wilderness filled up with rain and fine conversation with Ryan." This is his way and the benevolent gesture of his hand has me move up onto the bow platform. I cast and cast as the boat drifts into fog.

Soon it comes to me that casting while drifting down the estuary is casting blind — one cannot see the fish. So I have them land me below The Junction. I pull myself up the clay bank onto the beaten grass. It is clear that the bear we see each time is one of incalculable habit, among fine deep grasses that bend with the wind. I am left an airhorn to hold up its advances and then the boat moves with its casual conversation into a curtain of mist and so from my sight.

My interest is not in vain. A few minutes after the wash subsides, fish begin nosing the sky once more. This is in the way that, in passing a spring pond, we create a silence among the frog voices and they take shape again, like a bell, after our passing. Here and then there and then repeating as rain, one after the other, salmon roll their dorsal surfaces. They are awake, interested, focussed outside their hormones.

I move down the slippery bottom. Wading boots and neoprenes would have come in handy. Soon I am over my depth, moving after the fish, gumboots full of water. I station myself in the shade of the fir tree, its roots in the mouth of No Name Creek, and softly cast the purple-and-white Clouser above so the stream will turn and straighten and sink the fly to the first fish in its station. If I am lucky I will be able to draw it off, then sequentially fish the pool so I do not scare the downstream ones. In this way I will catch more than had I moved right into their main density.

My strategy proves itself as soon a fine, ocean blue buck — not of the camouflage green-and-white colouration, the grotesque Hunchback of Notre Dame back — whacks the fly. No kype, no sea lice, all the silver a fly fishermen likes. And then another, and another, all perfect replicas. Finally a boat is sent for me, and interrupts my passion for catching and releasing every fish in the pool.

Back at the lodge I am turning down my slickers and slipping out of my wet pants and socks. Terri is at the cleaning bench with his gear in front of him. And then he turns to me.

"Did you put this here?"

"I am sorry, I do not follow you."

"This reel. I put all my gear out and when I returned with a soft towel, this reel – it is the one you lost, Dennis."

I am dumbfounded. My bad and good luck are inseparable on this trip.

"Did you give this to me? I have no memory of this."

"I don't either. Let's call it a miracle."

"It must be."

Karma, serendipity, call it what you will — in city or where there are no people. We have found our luck in catching fish. We have indicated many flies, and left digital images for Michael to consider. There are plans for Tasu: pontoon boats for the approach waters; a flats boat from the tropics with a pole for the estuaries; fibreglass ones with smoothed-out casting platforms; and a jetboat for the river.

Why do I return to the fish? I think it is the gamble. You put down your bet and then you wait. When you are fortunate you are rewarded. The excitement of holding a wilderness beauty is the lure for the angler. I remember Haig-Brown had a similar conception of the reason a man or woman will come to the fish. I believe he put it like this though I cannot be certain of the writing from which it comes: "I should not be so excited when a little trout of perhaps three pounds comes to my fly, but I cannot help but say that I am."

I did not realize that karma and my approach — of giving thanks — were one and the same until here they came to me. I did not express this personally to Terri. Perhaps by this writing I have had the chance to right the wrong of callous words. I did not think to express the same to the rod I did not lose nor to the reel that came back to me. All things must end and we will be there to face them. Chopper blades beat the air. It seems they always do.

Appendix : Lodges

Charlotte Princess, Oak Bay Marine Group, Victoria, www.obmg.com, 1-800-663-7090 (Martin Paish).

Hakai Pass Beach Resort, Smithers, www.hakai.com, 1-800-668-3474.

Island West Resort, Ucluelet, www.islandwestresort.com, 1-250-726-7515 (Norm Reite).

Jack's Place, Port Alberni, www.hawkeyemarinegroup.com, 1-800-293-0468.

Marabell, Oak Bay Marine Group, Victoria, www.obmg.com, 1-800-663-7090 (Martin Paish).

Trailhead Resort, Port Renfrew, www.trailhead-resort.com, 1-250-647-5468 (Peter Hovey).

Tyee Resort, Bamfield, www.tyeeresort.com, 1-888-493-8933 (Liz Johnston).

Weigh West Resort, Tofino, www.weighwest.com, 1-800-665-8922 (Shawn Bennett).

West Coast Resorts: Lodge at Tasu Sound (Mike Coyne), Englefield Bay Lodge and Redfern River Lodge (Peter Bueschkens), Richmond, www.westcoastresorts.com, 1-800-810-8933 (Sarah-Jane Coe, Wendy Oppelt).

Wilp Syoon, www.wilpsyoon.com, 1-800-596-2226 (Ken Bejcar).